Interpreters
in
Public Services:
Policy and Training

Phil Baker with Zahida Hussain

and Jane Saunders

Publisher Jo Campling

Published in association with the Further Education Unit

Venture Press

Published by Venture Press
16 Kent Street
Birmingham B5 6RD

First published 1991

Design and production by Saxon Publishing Consultants Limited
Typeset in 10/11 Baskerville by TecSet Limited

Printed and Bound in Great Britain by
Hartnolls Limited, Bodmin, Cornwall.

ISBN 0–90010–2–79 9

Acknowledgements

We would like to thank the following for their perceptions and support:

The Further Education Unit, in particular Dr Dennis Drysdale, Alan Murray and David Thomas (PICKUP), staff and clients of Southall Social Services office, and in particular Myra Douglas, Amarjit Kanth, Sushil Bhagat, Madan Singh, and Santokh Singh Ghai; student interpreters on two Diploma courses in Community Interpreting, where the approach to interpreter training was developed; the ADSS, the local authority Social Services departments and the Community Relations Councils who assisted with background research; Charles Lewis for designing the computer programme and Neghat Lakdawala for assisting with processing; Daphne Crossfield, Anita Sturch and Monica Crossfield for the many hours of typing which led to the final version; Kamaljit Kaur Gill for her assistance with client interviews; Jane Shackman and Bergeas Khalid for valuable advice and assistance; and in particular the authors would like to thank Amarjit Khera for insights drawn from years of experience in the Southall community.

Glossary

ADSS	Association of Directors of Social Services
ALBSU	Adult Literacy and Basic Skills Unit
BASW	British Association of Social Workers
CAB	Citizens Advice Bureau
CCETSW	Central Council for Education and Training in Social Work
CP	Community Programme (later replaced by ET – see below.)
CRC	Community Relations Council
CRE	Commission for Racial Equality
ESL	English as a Second Language
ET	Employment Training
ILT	Industrial Language Training
LA	Local Authority
LEA	Local Education Authority
LMP	Linguistic Minorities Project
MSC	Manpower Services Commission (replaced by TA – see below)
NACRO	National Association for the Care and Resettlement of Offenders
NISW	National Institute of Social Work
PSI	Policy Studies Institute
TA	Training Agency (part of the Department of Employment)

Abbreviations following quotations in the text refer to the Bibliography (p.000 ff)

Contents

Conclusions

Preface

Using interpreters is nothing new, nor is the interpreting profession. As international relationships, whether political, economic or social have developed and the need for better communication across the boundaries of language has emerged, interpreting has established itself as a valuable resource and as a useful profession. In terms of status and remuneration, interpreting is an attractive enterprise for many wishing to be interpreters, well acknowledged and appreciated by many others who use their services.

The international status of the interpreting profession is hardly reflected or represented in Social Services and other related agencies. Unfortunately the language barrier has been one of the most oppressive factors in denying many black and minority ethnic families their right to services, simply because the service agencies are not able to communicate with them in their own languages. Even when service providers have attempted to overcome their linguistic shortcomings by, for example, getting someone to interpret, the forces of language, race and power have determined both the quality of interpreting and its outcome. In the absence of institutional acknowledgement and professional recognition of the role and status of interpreting, more often than not interpreting in minority community languages has remained cheap, ineffective and inadequate to the detriment of black and minority ethnic individuals and families in need of service.

I am therefore delighted to see this book being published. It is long awaited and long overdue. I am confident that it has the capacity to raise the awareness of service providers and assist them in establishing interpreting services.

Apart from giving examples of interpreting initiatives, the authors have addressed some of the most crucial issues which merit the attention of service agencies and their professional. They stress the continuing need for interpreting services, and justify such services within the context of legal obligations and good practice. There is much to learn from this book for all planners and providers of services in multi-ethnic Britain.

Linguistic skill is an essential prerequisite of social work and other caring professions, without which they can neither communicate nor provide an effective and sensitive service. Not speaking the language of the user/client then is the problem of professionals, not of users or clients. However, it becomes the problem for users and clients, when their legitimate access to adequate services is denied due to lack of language provision – when they get trapped in the power dynamics of language and ethnicity, which perpetuate racism and oppression. It is a professional duty to protect the interests of users and clients, and to promote the welfare of the most vulnerable members of our communities. An interpretation service is one of the aids to enable service planners and providers to fulfill their responsibilities. This book can assist the enabling process.

BANDANA AHMED
Director
Race Equality Unit
National Institute for Social Work

Introduction

Signposts for Policy Development

An increasing number of public authorities serving multi-racial communities are acknowledging the need to employ interpreters, in order to meet statutory obligations and provide an effective and equitable service to members of the public whose English is limited.

This has coincided with the adoption of formal equal opportunities policies by many authorities and with the growing realisation that keeping records of the ethnic origin of staff and clients is an essential pre-requisite for monitoring the extent to which these policies are put into practice.

The employment of interpreters as permanent staff is for some authorities a recent innovation and for the majority of those serving a multi-lingual public an issue which either is, or, in the authors' view, should be currently under consideration. As often happens when policy is at an early stage in its development, there is considerable variation in the forms of provision chosen. Some authorities have hesitated to make provision because of the absence of tried and tested models.

Drawing on a survey of practice in 51 local authorities, this book aims to assist authorities to decide what form of provision would be most appropriate in the context of local conditions. It also identifies organisational factors which can make interpreting provision more or less effective in contributing to the achievement of an authority's overall equal opportunity objectives.

Developing Training

The training of community language interpreters, and of the staff who use their services, is also a recent development. For years interpreting was undertaken on an *ad hoc* – usually voluntary – basis by individuals in the community. Many public authorities still rely on sessional interpreters but are becoming aware of the dangers inherent in an unstructured approach – particularly where relatives or children are used – and of the advantages of employing permanent in-house interpreters where appropriate. There is also a growing recognition of the fact that there is more to interpreting than simply being able to speak English and another language, and that working through an interpreter also involves skills which do not necessarily come naturally. There is an increasing demand for:

1) Professional training for community language interpreters which leads to a recognised qualification.

2) In-service training for staff who work through interpreters in order to communicate effectively with members of the public who have limited English.

This book examines the kinds of training currently available to both groups and make recommendations for further development.

Scope of the Book

This book will be relevant to managers and service providers in a wide range of statutory contexts – from health and social services, housing, education, social security to the probation service, the police and the courts.

It will also be useful to voluntary and community organisations – both to those who are providing or want to provide interpreting services themselves and to those who want to initiate a dialogue with public authorities in their area about the provision of interpreting services.

The book also has implications for Further and Higher Education colleges who provide training courses for local authorities and for members of the community. Attention is given, for example to the content of professional social work courses as well as to post-qualification training for social workers. It is also hoped that the book will prompt more colleges with expertise in language and communication skills to develop courses leading to professional qualifications for interpreters.

Interpreting and Race

Although interpreting is an issue for all the linguistic minority groups in Britain, it does not necessarily affect them all in the same way. In particular, people with limited English who are also members of racial minorities may be doubly disadvantaged, and it is this which often distinguishes the experience of, for instance, members of the Polish community from that of their South Asian counterparts. White speakers of English born in Britain may use perceptions such as 'they've been in this country for years but they still haven't learnt English properly' as rationalisations for racial prejudice. And an inability to negotiate effectively in a language which is not their own can make members of racial minorities even more vulnerable to institutional racism than would otherwise be the case. Particular attention is therefore given to this aspect of the subject.

It is important to recognise that a broader concept of interpreting may also apply in some circumstances to black people of West Indian origin. The fact that their language is English-based may mean that they are forced to 'standardise' their English when communicating with white officers in public services, with a corresponding reduction in their ability to express feelings or concepts. Further work remains to be done in this important area.

Chapter 1

From Reaction to Recognition

In this chapter we trace the changes in public attitudes and policy towards linguistic minorities which have taken place since the sixties. The purpose of the chapter is to define 'where we are now' by pinpointing factors which prevented the development of equitable policies on interpreting in the sixties and seventies and the significant factors which have led us to the current widespread recognition of the need for public provision of interpreting services.

Obstacles to Policy Development

The Initial Reaction: English Classes for Adults

The fact that many of the Asian and other ethnic minority groups who came to Britain in the sixties and early seventies were not fluent in English was well-known. In 1966 the Local Government Act made extra resources available to local authorities in respect of additional staff appointments or of increased work loads, arising out of the presence within their areas of Commonwealth immigrants having a different language or culture from the rest of the community. This recognition of the need for local authorities to make a specific response was also reflected in the Plowden Report's (1967) proposals for the setting up of Education Priority Areas on criteria which included the proportion of children in the Local Education Authority (LEA) concerned who needed special English teaching.

However, the immediate nature of the problem which non-English speaking children presented for their indigenous teachers had the effect of obscuring the need their parents also had to learn English. LEAs' duties under the Education Act meant that even reluctant local authorities had to address the needs of children with limited English. But there was no such duty in relation to ethnic minority adults who wanted to learn the language. The point was succinctly put by the Select Committee on Race Relations and Immigration in its comments on Further Education for immigrants:

'Resources are limited. We frequently urge the provision of increased facilities for the education of immigrant children. We believe this is the right area on which to concentrate, the younger, the better. It would be unrealistic to suggest that statutory bodies should do this and at the same time make a massive contribution to adult education . . . Furthermore, because of working hours and social arrangements, statutory bodies would find it difficult to cope with the infinite variety of time and method needed for the education of adult immigrants. This is a specially fruitful field for voluntary bodies and industry.' (SCRRI 1973 – p.35)

Apart from a few local authorities who experimented with adult education classes in English, the initiative was therefore left largely to minority groups such as religious centres or the Indian and Pakistani Workers Associations, a few branches of the Workers Education Association, and the Community Relations Commission established under the 1968 Race Relations Act.

Local Community Relations Councils (CRCs) began voluntary language schemes 'to assist Asian women to overcome the isolation caused by their inability to speak English'. Staffed by housewives, student teachers and in some instances, sixth-formers, as well as by qualified teachers, these schemes provided mainly one-to-one tuition in the home. By 1973 the Community Relations Commission reported over seventy such schemes in operation throughout the country. (CRC, 1973).

However, schemes of this kind were unable to reach the majority of Asian men and a large proportion of women who were in full time work, often working long shifts which made attendance at English classes impossible. An Industrial Language Training Unit was established at the Pathway Further Education Centre, Southall, and employers were persuaded to release Asian and other ethnic minority workers to attend classes, in the workplace, in paid time. Encouraged by positive remarks made about the scheme by the Parliamentary Select Committee, several other LEAs set up Industrial Language Training Units similar to the one at Pathway, mostly funded under Section 11. In 1975, John Frazer, Under-Secretary of State for Employment, said that 'the government recognises that the only fully satisfactory point at which language training can be given to the majority of people with jobs is at the workplace, and recognise that action is needed on a national basis'. (NCILT, 1976). Discussions were initiated between LEAs and central government which led to the establishment of the national Industrial Language Training (ILT) scheme, eventually funded, in 1978, by the Manpower Services Commission and consisting of units in twenty-six local authorities.

A further initiative in the early seventies was the establishment of literary and numeracy courses in colleges of further education, funded by the Training Services Agency. Take up among Asians was high, but these courses still only reached a tiny minority of those who needed them. The scheme was mainly designed for the unemployed and could not reach the great majority who were at work.

The lack of real progress in the seventies was highlighted in 1981, when the Home Affairs Committee (HAC) published *Racial Disadvantage*, the report of an inquiry 'undertaken against a background of concern at the state of race relations in the United Kingdom.' Among its wide-ranging and often penetrative findings was the following statement:

'Language and communication problems emerge in every area of public policy from pre-primary education to the care of the elderly. Yet there is no government programme and no overall government responsibility for conquering this far from insuperable disadvantage. The Manpower Services Commission fund some language training of those at work through Industrial Language Training Units and through TOPS courses. The Department of Education and Science oversee LEA arrangements for teaching children. A network of local voluntary bodies has grown up trying valiantly to meet local expressions of need. Nor has there ever been a thorough and far-reaching examination of the teaching of English as a second language to those settled here, both adults and children. *We recommend that the Government establish such an inquiry, to report on the steps which could be taken to ensure that all those entitled here with low oral and written English language skills have adequate access to language training.*' (HAC, 1981 para. 33).

The government declined to undertake an inquiry, although it accepted the importance of providing adults with the opportunity to learn English. The main thrust of public policy at national level continued to be aimed at the education of children.

The Home Affairs Committee also recommended that the government explore the possibility of further funding to persuade employers to make more use of the Industrial Language Training scheme. The official government reply to this was non committal and although some expansion of the scheme took place, the impact made on communication skills by ILT units remained much smaller than it could have been had realistic funding been available. MSC's contribution to ILT costs rose from £1.8 million in 1980 to just under £2 million in 1985, but over this period the scheme's staff (approx. a hundred)provided language and communication training for only thirteen thousand six hundred and eighty speakers of English as a second language (MSC, 1986). This was a drop in the ocean, when set against a 1978 estimate that there had been at that time, over two hundred thousand adults in Britain who spoke English slightly or not at all. (CRE, NCILT, 1978).

The continuing low priority afforded by central government to English as a Second Language (ESL) for adults in the eighties is also reflected in Section 11 expenditure. The Home Office estimated that in mid 1988 approximately four hundred teachers of ESL for adults were being funded under Section 11, in contrast to two thousand school-based teachers. In the context of a national total of some twelve thousand Section 11 funded posts, the amount being spent on adult ESL remained very small. The contribution made by MSC programmes for the unemployed was equally small. In 1986/87, for example, over nine thousand ethnic minority people received help under the Wider Opportunities Training Programme, but fewer than fifteen hundred received any kind of ESL teaching, reflecting the fact that participation in these programmes was predominantly by younger people.

The unsatisfactory nature of this situation was again highlighted by the Home Affairs Committee in 1986, in its report on the Bangladeshi community. It was considered 'a matter of national importance' that those with little or no English should be given the opportunity to learn it, and the Committee found it unacceptable that there should be areas where such opportunities were not available. The situation was felt to be so serious that the Committee recommended that:

1) There should be a statutory duty on LEAs to make ESL teaching available to all those in need of it who request it.

2) That LEAs give financial and other support to ESL classes organised by Bangladeshis or other ethnic minorities for their own community. (HAC, 1986 – paras. 60 and 61).

As in 1981, the government failed to respond in any meaningful way. It was left to individual LEAs to 'decide on the extent of their provision in the light of locally identified needs and priorities'. (GR, 1987 p. 9).

Part of the underlying rationale for the continuing under-resourcing of ESL provision for adults has been the widespread belief that the problem would 'solve itself' as minority communities became more established and their levels of English improved through day to day contract with the majority population. In fact, research indicates that there has been only a relatively small improvement in levels of English among those with the most limited communication ability

The Policy Studies Institute's 1981 survey *Black and White Britain* found that the proportions of Asian men speaking English 'slightly or not at all' had only decreased from 30% to 23% since its previous survey in 1974. 59% of Asian women had spoken English slightly or not at all in 1974, and this had only decreased to 52% by 1981. The slow rate of improvement over time has been underlined by the 1989 survey of speakers of English as a second language carried out by the Adult Literacy and Basic Skills Unit. Based on over a thousand interviews mainly with Asian people but also covering speakers of fifty other minority languages the survey found that 29% of respondents spoke English only a little or not at all. (Men: 18%; Women: 40%). We explore the factors affecting language acquisition in Chapter 2.

Faced with the day-to-day experience of dealing with members of the public with limited English, and the absence of a more adequate public strategy for teaching English to adults, it seems reasonable to expect that public bodies would have invested some resources in interpreting.

There is evidence that this began to happen in the early 1980s – for example:

1) Leicestershire Social Services department established a budget for sessional interpreters in 1980, to meet the demand from the Asian and Eastern European communities. It provided sixty-six sessions in its first year, one hundred and thirty-two sessions in 1981 and two hundred and sixteen sessions in 1982.

2) In the same year Strathclyde Regional Council supported an Urban Aid application from Strathclyde CRC to run an interpreting service. Approval was given and by 1982/3 the service was undertaking over fifteen hundred interpreting sessions per annum, and in addition, several hundred document translations.

These were among the earliest initiatives taken by local authorities to provide interpreting services. The reasons why they did not occur much earlier, and in greater numbers, are explored below.

Social Attitudes

Britain's first, hesitant steps towards antidiscrimination law in 1965 were widely criticised as having made little difference to the widespread discrimination in housing and employment suffered by black people. Paradoxically, two of the half dozen legal prosecutions were against black community leaders. While the 1968 Act extended coverage to commercial transactions and included a blanket prohibition on racially discriminatory advertisements, it was enacted against the background of restrictive immigration legislation aimed at limiting the entry rights of East African Asians from Kenya. Enoch Powell made his notorious 'rivers of blood' speech in April 1968, exploiting the resentment felt by a proportion of the indigenous white population at the growth of Asian communities in Britain. 'Although he was dismissed from the Shadow Cabinet . . . Mr. Powell was clearly speaking a popular view'. (Claiborne, 1974 p. 12.) Attitudes at the time are well documented in E. J. B. Rose's classic study *Colour and Citizenship* (1969).

It is symptomatic of the political tensions which existed that policy studies of the time were frequently addressed to the 'problem' of 'special provision' for ethnic minorities. In spite of increased evidence of continuing racial discrimination and of economic and social need in the areas where Asians had settled, there was a fear that specific allocation of extra resources to meet these needs would give an 'unfair advantage' to the immigrants in relation to the white community. This was allied with an often expressed belief that the way to be fair was to treat everyone exactly the same, irrespective of race. Birmingham City Council were quoted in the Cullingworth Report, for instance, as stating that 'The Council has always insisted upon immigrant families being treated in precisely the same way as everyone else'. (MHLG, 1969 p. 122). Underlying this concern was also a less frequently expressed worry that special provisions for black people would in some way draw attention to them and fuel the prejudices of which policy-makers, whatever their personal views, were only too well aware.

It is therefore perhaps not surprising that none of the major reports on local authority services which appeared in the sixties mentioned interpreting provision as an appropriate use of either Section 11 or Urban Aid funds. The onus for communication about service entitlement was placed firmly with the immigrant. It was up to him or her to learn English (although it was not generally seen as part of the LEA's duties to assist in this) or to provide his or her own interpreter from the community.

Similar attitudes were reflected in public policies well into the seventies. For instance, research carried out for the Community Relations Commission between 1974 and 1976 produced statements such as the following:

'It is very hard to say we are going to provide things for ethnic minorities without creating a very real feeling amongst the indigenous population that to have something which excludes them is wrong, it's not a fair world, it's an immigrant's world ... In x (an area of ethnic concentration) there are a lot of people who have lived there all their lives and they complain very bitterly that they are strangers in their own land. And if we start putting facilities which are for the immigrant community only, we feed this discontent and I am not sure in the long run we do anything to further the cause of racial integration.' (Quoted from a local authority Social Services department in CRC, 1977 p. 47).

The Select Committee on Race Relations and Immigration reported that in the borough of Haringey

'an area where careers assistance presented a special problem because of the immigrant population ... had rejected the idea of making arrangements for special ethnic groups in their careers guidance service, because as well as being difficult, "it might be construed as discrimination, albeit of a positive nature" '.

They made it a deliberate feature of policy that 'the amount of help to indigenous and immigrant applicants should be the same.' (SCRRI, 1973 p.18).

This is not to say that local or central government did treat everyone the same all the time or in every respect. The doctrine often appeared to be applied somewhat selectively – for example, policies aimed at making immigrants less visible through dispersal were pursued with some vigour. 'Dispersal of immigrant concentrations should be regarded as a desirable consequence, but not the overriding purpose, of housing individual families on Council estates' wrote the Cullingworth commitee (MHLG 1969 p. 136). While it rejected the compulsory dispersal of black people, the Committee described dispersal 'with full respect for the wishes of the people concerned' as a 'laudable aim of policy'. In 1965 the government had given similar advice to LEAs when it stated that:

'above one-third of immigrant children is the maximum that is normally acceptable in a school if social strains are to be avoided and educational standards maintained. Local Educational Authorities are advised to arrange for the dispersal of immigrant children over a greater number of schools. (Cmnd 2739, para. 42).

In spite of indications that 'bussing' might be illegal under the 1968 Race Relations Act and the strong feelings of black parents who found the practice objectionable dispersal policies in education persisted well into the seventies.

Dispersal policies were a symptom of the widespread belief in 'assimilation' as the solution to the 'problem' posed by black immigration to the indigenous population. Assimilation may be defined as the reduction and, if possible, the elimination of any cultural or behavioural features of the ethnic minority communities which differentiated them from the white majority. The responsibility for this adaptation process was assumed to rest with the immigrant, but she or he could be helped by social policies aimed at 'mixing them in' with the majority. This approach had been rejected as early as 1966 by Roy Jenkins, Home Secretary, in preference for the word 'integration': 'not as a flattening process of assimilation, but equal opportunity accompanied by cultural diversity, in an atmosphere of mutual tolerance'. (Jenkins, 1966). But in the seventies it would appear that there were still many who hoped for such a 'flattening process'.

In this context, the provision of an interpreter from public funds would have implied acceptance of language difference as a fact – and, by implication, the acceptance of other aspects of cultural and behavioural difference as more than simply temporary factors in a process of adjustment. It would have represented an accommodation by the white majority to a feature of the immigrant community which many whites assumed or hoped would disappear, namely a separate mother tongue.

The responsibility for providing interpreters was therefore left with the Asian community. The efforts of family and friends as ad hoc interpreters in countless situations were all that ensured that Asian people not fluent in English received at least some of the services they needed or were entitled to.

In general, public policy ignored the need for full-time interpreters, paid from public resources and available at the point where services were provided, until the early nineteen eighties.

Seebohm Re-Organisation and Economic Recession

For local authority Social Services, the period between 1970 and 1976 was one of hope and disappointment. In 1968, the Seebohm Report had made far-reaching recommendations for 'a new local authority department, providing a community-based and family-orientated service, which would be available to all'. As far as possible, a family or individual in need would be served by a single social worker, based in an area team, rather than by a number of officials with different specialisms and roles.

Following the Local Authority Social Services Act 1970, there was an initial increase in social services expenditure as the new, larger departments were set up and service re-organised – an average of 10% or more per year in real terms for the first few years. In 1974 further re-structuring led to the transfer of health service social workers to local authority social work departments. However, the economic recession which followed the oil crisis led to a significant cutback in growth in the second half of the decade. The rise in unemployment led to an increase in the demands being made on the (relatively new) Social Services departments, just at the time when resources began to be reduced. In addition, the upheaval caused by the structural changes and the rapid expansion of services affected the morale and pattern of work of social workers.

'The expansion of departments meant that many social workers were rapidly promoted to positions of supervision or management: the management training and experience available to departments was limited. These promotions meant that social workers in immediate contact with clients tended to be the less experienced or the less able.' (NISW, 1987 p.108).

In this context, the following comments made by social workers in 1977, in response to the CRE's first inquiry into social services provision after the 1976 Act, are perhaps not surprising:

'There is a danger in revealing needs when we do not have means to meet a stimulated demand. If people have a high expectation of service when you have few resources, they think you do not care . . . If we go too far in chasing up immigrants, it means that some other group in need will miss out.

With the black population . . . we could go in providing play-groups and day nurseries as long as we like and never satisfy the need. One of the difficulties of course is that the moment you do this as an authority it becomes not so much a support as an expected thing.' (CRC, 1977 p.55).

In the early part of the seventies Social Services managers had been preoccupied with the re-organisation and structure of departments and priorities for allocation of resources rather than matters of social work practice. By the second half of the decade 'the combined pressures of an unfavourable economic climate and growing demands had rendered local authority social workers sometimes incapable of meeting the authority's statutory obligations, let alone pursuing discretionary powers'. (NISW, 1982 p.108).

In a context where the prevailing ethos of service delivery in the sixties had been against targetting where black people were concerned, and re-organisation and recession together restricted the scope for a reappraisal of this approach, it is not surprising that any special needs of black clients with limited English were marginalised and that the particular need for interpreters was ignored or left to community initiatives. It was also to be expected that Social Services departments in multi-racial areas would be unprepared to respond immediately to the implications of the 1976 Race Relations Act.

Helping Factors

Effect of the 1976 Race Relations Act

The social context in which the Act was passed underlined the need for legislative reform. The Immigration Act of 1971 had not confirmed the claims made by some politicians that it would quiet the fears of the indigenous population about large-scale immigration. The arrival of refugees from Uganda and Malawi had been met with a 'media panic' which the growing National Front had been able to exploit to its advantage. Whereas the Front's formation in 1967, as a union of the British National Party and the League of Empire Loyalists had been almost totally ignored by press and public alike, by 1977 it had twenty-three branches and an estimated membership of between four thousand five hundred and six thousand (Taylor, 1977). The oil crisis had brought recession, and in August 1975 over a million people had registered as unemployed, for the first time since the war. Between 1973 and 1975, unemployment among black people had risen nearly two and a half times as fast as among the general population. Although the electoral success of the National Front was on the decline in the eighties, it gave frightening legitimacy to racist scapegoating, and probably contributed to the rise in racial attacks in the second half of the decade. (see Fryer, 1984 p. 395). In 1976, the year of the new Race Relations Act, Gurdip Singh Chagger, aged eighteen, was stabbed to death in Southall by a gang of white youths.

In spite of this unpromising context for the new legislation, it did mark a significant step forward for Asian and other black linguistic minorities in Britain. For the first time, positive action was given a legal basis. Section 71 placed a duty on local authorities to ensure that their functions were carried out 'with due regard to the need to eliminate unlawful discrimination and to promote equality of opportunity and good relations between persons of different racial groups'. Section 35 allowed provision to be made for the special needs of racial groups in education, training and welfare. Section 5 allowed selection on racial grounds where the post justified this as a 'genuine occupational qualification', and Section 38 permitted the provision of training and encouragement for members of racial minorities to take jobs in which their group had previously been under-represented.

The Act placed the previously controversial concept of 'special provision' within a legal framework. Not only did it remove any doubts policy-makers may have had about the legality of employing inter-preters to ensure that services were equally available to all sections of the community, but Section 71 placed a duty on local authorities to ensure that this was so, and the new Commission for Racial Equality had powers of investigation, to check on implementation.

In addition, the new Act re-defined discrimination in terms of (S.1.).

1) *Direct discrimination*: treating a person, on racial grounds, less favourably than others in the same or similar circumstances.

2) *Indirect discrimination*: applying a requirement or condition which, although applied equally to persons of all racial groups, is such that a considerably smaller proportion of a particular racial group can comply with it – and it cannot be shown to be justifiable on other than racial grounds.

The new concept of indirect discrimination had important implications where the provision of interpreters was concerned. It could be argued that a local authority which applied a requirement to communicate in English equally to all racial groups using its services would be discriminating, because a considerably smaller proportion of black linguistic minority groups would be able to comply with it. An Asian client, for example, who failed to receive a service to which he was entitled because of mis-communication, where no interpreter was available, could claim that the local authority had failed in its duties under the Act.

The new responsibilities placed on local authorities by the Act also began to prompt a reassessment, slow at first, of the value of ethnic monitoring.

Research carried out for the Community Relations Commission in the two years before the 1976 Race Relations Act, in eight multi-racial areas, had found that it was very rare for Social Service Committees to have discussed the needs of minorities. Research carried out for the SSRC during the same period, but over a wider area had confirmed that most Social Services departments did not maintain separate ethnic records. (Jones, 1977). This meant that there was no systematic way of assessing the extent to which the services available were meeting ethnic minority needs.

By 1978 the situation had begun to improve slightly – it is reasonable to assume, as a result of the 1976 Act. A survey of sixty-two local authority Social Services departments found that seven now kept systematic records of ethnic minority clients and a further seven were considering doing so. However, about 75% still kept no ethnic records and the survey report, produced by a joint working party of the CRE and the Association of Directors of Social Services, expressed disquiet at the situation.

'We are dismayed by the lack of information about the current need and provision in relation to black communities and uncertainties about how best to approach new communities. We are convinced that ignorance is no basis for policy development, implementation and evaluation and stress the need for departments to keep records of staff and clients in order to *monitor* both staffing and practices.' (ADSS/CRE, 1978 – original italics).

Apart from the lack of data on clients the ADSS/CRE report found that almost 90% of the departments surveyed kept no systematic ethnic records of staff, and no information was apparently received as to why this was so. This meant that staffing policy was still largely invisible to scrutiny and any targetting of posts was bound to be done in an *ad hoc* manner, rather than as part of a corporate strategy. (ADSS/CRE, 1978 p.14). Before a social services department could take the decision to employ an interpreter on a full-time basis, a case for resource allocation needed to be made, on the basis of figures (or at least informed estimates) giving, for instance:

1) The proportion of staff able to communicate with clients in languages other than English.
2) The proportions of clients using family, friends or community organisations to interpret.
3) The preferences of clients re choice of interpreter.
4) Comparisons of social need indicators in the community with take-up of services.

Without the collection of basic data on ethnic origins of staff and clients, such a case could not be made and it is therefore not surprising that in the four years following the 1976 Act, interpreting continued to be provided in the main through clients' own efforts, or not at all. It seems likely that the introduction of ethnic monitoring procedures would have continued at what was, relatively, a snail's pace if the need for more rapid change had not been highlighted by social unrest at the turn of the decade.

Social Unrest in Black Communities (79/81) and the Government's Response

It took time for the newly created Commission for Racial Equality to find its feet. Between 1978 and 1982 the CRE carried out an investigation of Hackney housing department's allocations policy, but the Non-Discrimination notice was not actually served until June 1983, recommending among other things, the keeping of ethnic records and monitoring. (CRE, 1984 p.5.).

In the meantime, however, policy-making received a sharp nudge forward as a result of the urban 'troubles' 1979–81. For the Asian communities, the first of these, in 1979, was particularly significant.

On 23 April the National Front insisted on holding an 'election meeting' in Southall, home of Britain's largest Sikh community. The latter responded with a non-violent gathering in the streets which involved some five thousand people in a peaceful protest against Ealing Council's decision to allow the meeting – perceived by the community as a deliberate insult – to go ahead. The Home Secretary's response was to draft in two thousand seven hundred and fifty-six (2,756) police who broke up the gathering, arresting seven hundred people, three hundred and forty-two of whom were charged. The methods used by some of the police, including the Special Patrol Group, led to several hundred people being injured, and, it is widely believed, to the death of Blair Peach, one of the demonstrators, (Southall Rights, 1980).

These events had a profound effect on the relationship between Britain's Asian Communities and their local authorities, not just in Ealing, but throughout the country. They highlighted the extent of the gap in perceptions which existed between the two, and the extent to which local authority decision making could be out of step with the views of the Asian electorate. They also marked the beginning of a new assertiveness on the part of the Asian communities, a shift from a passive relationship with public authority to an assertion of their rights as citizens. And they gave a new significance to the duty to promote good relations between persons of different racial groups, placed on local authorities by S.71 of the Race Relations Act.

The message was reinforced, although in a different way, by the disturbances which occurred during the next two years in Brixton, Toxteth and elsewhere (and in Southall again in 1981). The dissatisfaction with public policies felt by the black communities was placed firmly on the agendas of both local and national government. In his report on the Brixton disorders, Lord Scarman concluded that 'urgent action is needed if racial disadvantage is not to become an endemic, ineradicable disease threatening the very survival of our society.' (Scarman, 1981).

In 1981 the Home Affairs Committee report (Racial Disadvantage) provided important confirmation of the point made by the CRE and ADSS in 1978 about the lack of data on ethnic origins. The committee complained that it was 'impossible to discover the simple factual truth about some of the most significant and apparently straightforward matters . . . inspired guesswork and extrapolation from old and often unreliable national figures is reflected on a local scale often accompanied by controversy and exaggeration'. (HAC, 1981 para. 8.). One of the Committee's main recommendations was that public authorities should institute ethnic monitoring of the services they provided. The government accepted the recommendation in respect of the Civil Service and the latter subsequently adopted formal equal opportunity policies on race and gender (December 1984) and began a phased programme of ethnic monitoring which was completed in 1988. Guarded approval, subject to consultation with the local authority associations, was also given to the principle of ethnic monitoring by local Councils. The government's formal reply to the report acknowledged that 'it is only in the light of such information that appropriate steps can be taken to remedy racial disadvantage'. (Cmnd 8476, 1981 p.5.)

Two years later, a joint government/local authority working party listed the arguments in favour of monitoring origins of both staff and clients:

1) They enable an authority to be factually informed in order to accept or refute allegations of racial discrimination.
2) They provide a basis for policy formulation and planning of programmes.
3) They highlight patterns of discrimination which might have occurred unintentionally but nevertheless leave particular racial groups disadvantaged.
4) require different responses in service provision.
5. They provide a basis on which an authority can monitor the effects of its policies on different racial groups and also assess whether or not its race relations policies are being successfully implemented. (DOE, 1983 p.19.).

Gradually, increasing numbers of Councils began to introduce ethnic records in the second half of the eighties.

Pathway's 1988 survey of local authority Social Services departments (described in more detail in Chapter 5) provides an interesting comparison with the 1978 ADSS/CRE survey. The results of each are given in Table 1.1.

Table 1.1 Local Authorities Monitoring Ethnic Origins of Staff and Clients

	Staff		Clients	
Surveys	No.	%	No.	%
1978 ADSS/CRE survey (n = 62)	3	5	7	11
1988 Pathway survey (n = 51)	25	49	18	35

In ten years, the proportion of local authorities monitoring the ethnic origin of staff had risen from 5% to near 50%. Monitoring of clients' ethnic origin had increased rather more slowly, but it was nevertheless more than three times the 1978 percentage.

The Use of Section 11 Funding

Thirteen of the twenty authorities in Pathway's survey who employed permanent interpreting staff did so with 75% funding received from the Home Office under Section 11 of the Local Government Act 1966. A 'snapshot' Home Office count in April 1988 placed Section 11 funding for interpreting nationally at seventy posts. Further applications for an unspecified number of local authorities were under consideration at the time.

Undoubtedly a contributing factor here is the encouragement given to local authorities by the specific listing of interpreters in Home Office circular 72/86 among the examples of the kinds of post which could be funded. This came at a time when there had been widespread criticism of the use made of Section 11 funding by local Councils. The circular set out new conditions for the funding of all Section 11 posts in an attempt to ensure that money allocated was being used specifically to meet the needs of 'people of Commonwealth origin whose language or culture of origin differed from those of the rest of the community.'

Strict monitoring by central government, including a 'rolling programme' of visits to local authorities to look in detail at the whole of their Section 11 provision was promised. However, this proved impossible to undertake effectively with the resources available and a further review of the administration of the scheme led to further tightening up of the grant criteria in 1990. Interpreting and translating posts, however, were again listed specifically as items for which application could be made, and the guidance issued contained frequent reference to the need to ensure that the 'language barrier' did not prevent ethnic minorities from obtaining equal access to services.

It is worth noting that the government remained concerned to review all projects regularly against 'recognisable performance targets'. This suggests much more rigourous record-keeping of the activities of Section 11 funded interpreters than was the case in the eighties. Pathway's survey found extremely patchy record-keeping, with some authorities noting simply the number of requests met and nothing more.

Policy Guidance on the Provision of Interpreters

The Section 11 guidance quoted above represents clear recognition by central government of the importance of language disadvantage and acceptance that both central and local government should share the cost of interpreting provision, although the extent of provision clearly depends on the cash limits imposed.

A number of other policy documents and reports stand out as milestones on the way to this point.

The major concerns voiced in these reports have been:

1) The effect of language disadvantage on take-up of services.
2) The questionable nature of ad hoc policies on interpreting which rely on community organisations, family, friends or school-age children.
3) The need for full-time professional interpreters employed by local authorities.
4) The link between effective communication and the right of the ethnic minority citizen to participate equally in British society.

All sponsored by local and national bodies, the reports are as follows:

24

1) *Multi-racial Britain: the Social Services response*
Produced in 1978 by a working party of members of the Association of Directors of Social Services and the Commission for Racial Equality. Wide-ranging and detailed recommendations for the DHSS, local authorities, CCETSW and the CRE, including that interpreters 'should be appointed on a full-time basis where there are language barriers'.

2) *Race Equality and Social Policy in London (1980)*
Discussion paper presented by the CRE to the London Boroughs Association. Stressed the need for local Councils to appoint interpreters to ensure that ethnic minority residents could 'not only make use of the services available but participate more fully in the wider life of the community'.

3) *Social Workers: their role and tasks (The 'Barclay report')*
This well-known report of a working group of the National Institute for Social Work contained some incisive comments on the effect of language disadvantage on the fair delivery of services. In particular, it was dismissive of the frequent reliance on Asian staff to interpret on an *ad hoc* basis:

> 'Asian workers told us that they found themslves all too often being pressed to act as interpreters. This cannot be a satisfactory practice. We recognise the difficulties of deployment if professional inter-preters are employed, but this must be the best arrangement. The difficulties can, we believe, be reduced if the social worker, though unfamiliar with the language, has at least a good grounding in the knowledge of the traditional way of life and customs which the client takes for granted' (para. 9.58)

The report went on to recommend the employment of specialist workers.

4) *Local authorities and Racial Disadvantage (1982)*
A discussion document produced by a joint government/local authority association working group set up following the government's response to the Home Affairs Committee's report on racial disadvantage. The group saw effective communication as essential for local democracy in multi-racial areas and noted that 'ethnic minority communities now argue forcefully that decisions must no longer be made on their behalf without their full involvement'. The appointment of interpreters in Council departments was recommended.

All of these reports represent both a contribution to and an expression of the growing awareness that interpreting provision is a mainstream local authority function in multi-racial areas.

Conclusion

Policy development in this area moved slowly in the seventies and early eighties, very much in line with the wider changes of attitude to race and ethnic relations in Britain in which gradually took place over the same period.

Progress was hampered by the lack of ethnic records about both clients and staff, which meant that for many years the information required to devise need-based policies and monitor their effectiveness was simply not available. Happily, this began to change towards the end of the eighties and the general trend shifted towards ethnic monitoring by public authorities serving multi-racial populations.

Initially, the teaching of English in schools, and the limited language teaching provision for adults had acted as a smokescreen, obscuring the immediate need for interpreting provision today with the promise of fluency in English tomorrow. By the end of the eighties, it was apparent that, far from being mutually exclusive, these two areas of public policy should go hand in hand.

The recognition of the importance of interpreting provision by local authorities – backed by 75% funding from central government which is embodied in the 1986 and 1990 Section 11 circulars is a reflection of a significant evolution of thinking at both local and national levels. In social policy terms, it has been perhaps a question of 'better late than never'. The fact that it took us twenty years or more to reach this point serves to underline the need to speed up the process in the nineties.

Chapter 2

The Continuing Need for Interpreting Services

"This man has been living here since
1965 and here we are in 1988 and he
still needs an interpreter. He says
he is British and has been in this
country for nearly a quarter of a
century. Why do we have to have an
interpreter in Panjabi to explain the
social security system to him?"

Judge Potter at Birmingham Crown Court – Reported in The Times – 6.5.88.

In this chapter we set out to answer the judge's question. We summarise the most recent evidence of the current need for interpreting services and the likelihood of a continuing need in the nineties.

To establish the national picture we draw on research carried out by three separate organissations:

1) The Policy Studies Institute (PSI: published in 1984 as *Black and White Britain*, this study included five thousand and one interviews with individual adults from three thousand and eighty-three separate black households. 67% of the interviews were with Asians from India, Pakistan, Bangladesh, Sri Lanka and East Africa. The report included information which brought up to date the previous PEP findings on fluency in English among the Asian population. (see p.00)

2) The Linguistic Minorities Project (LMP): published in 1985 *The Other Languages of England*, this was a language use survey carried out among twenty five hundred ethnic minority people in Coventry, Bradford and London. The survey was broader than PSI's and included speakers of Panjabi, Gujarati, Bengali, Greek, Italian, Polish, Portuguese, Turkish, Ukrainian and several Far Eastern languages.

3) The Adult Literacy and Basic Skills Unit (ALBSU) commissioned a survey from Research Resources Ltd (RRL) published in 1989 *Communication Skills among Non English First Language Speakers*. This study was based on interviews with one thousand and twenty-five people. 85% of these spoke either Panjabi, Gujarati, Urdu, Bengali or Hindi as their first language. The remaining 15% spoke between them over fifty different languages 'from Persian to Polish, from Swahili to Spanish and from Kurdish to Korean'.

From these and also from other sources, we examine the evidence of a strong link between communication difficulty and deprivation in terms of income, employment, housing and take-up of benefits and services, suggesting that if public service departments are to reach the most disadvantaged members of their communities, then the employment of interpreters in multi-racial areas is essential.

Finally, we examine some examples of local investigations into the need for interpreting provision and suggest practical ways in which the nature and extent of local needs can be established.

The Ability to Speak and Understand English: the National Picture

The authors of the 1989 ALBSU study estimated that there were between 1.6 and 1.8 million adults in Britain whose first language was not English. The extent to which these people might need an interpreter is indicated from the analysis below.

Table 2.1

Ability level (self-assessed)	Understanding %	Speaking %
Not at all	4	6
A little	22	23
Fairly well	21	20
Very well	30	30
Excellently	22	20

Source: ALBSU/RRL 1989 p.10.

These figures suggest that there were at least 400,000 people in Great Britain in 1989 who would benefit from the availability of an interpreting service.

In general, men spoke and understood English better than women, confirming similar findings from both the earlier PSI and LMP studies.

Table 2.2

Ability level (self-assessed)	Men (speaking %)	Women (speaking %)	Men (understanding %)	Women (understanding %)
Not at all	1	11	1	7
A little	17	29	15	29
Fairly well	25	15	25	18
Very well	35	26	34	26
Excellently	22	18	25	20

PSI's 1984 analysis had gone a stage further to produce the following 'hierarchy' in the ability of respondents to speak English:

Table 2.3 Percentage of Asian adults speaking little or no English

Asian Adults	Percentages %
Bangladeshi women	76
Pakistani women	70
Bangladeshi men	50
Indian women	42
Pakistani men	27
African Asian women	23
Indian men	15
African Asian men	13
Sri Lankan women	(4)
Sri Lankan men	(-)

These figures reflect primarily differences of culture, socio-economic background, education and status between the different groups and the opportunities open to them both in their countries of origin and in Britain. PSI found that the Asian community in Britain included substantial numbers of people who were very poorly educated, but also substantial numbers who were very well educated, and that the gulf between these groups was far wider than within the more homogeneous populations of West Indian and white people. At one end of the spectrum, 15% of Asian men had left school before the age of thirteen, and 32% of Asian women had either left before they were twelve or had no schooling. (This goes some way to explaining the gender imbalance in the table above). At the other end of the spectrum, nearly a quarter of Asian men continued their education into their twenties, compared to 7% of white men and 2% of West Indian men. (PSI, p.132). Further education did not however necessarily mean better jobs in Britain. Asian men with qualifications were found by PSI to be more frequently in the lower manual jobs than their white counterparts, and less frequently in non-manual jobs. (PSI, p.159). Many ended up working in situations where the need or opportunity to use English was minimal, with the result that 'examination English' used in English-medium schools abroad sometimes did not reach the fluency needed for day to day use in this country.

The 'hierarchy' presented in the above table does not necessarily indicate a reluctance to learn English – 38% of the Asian women interviewed by PSI expressed an interest in attending classes to improve their English and this rose to 46% when Bangladeshi men and women were considered together. However, the combination of family commitments, shiftwork, long working days and, for the women, housework, has reduced substantially the proportion of Asians who have been able to attend classes in their spare time. PSI found that only 10% of Asian men and women had been able to attend classes, and that there was little correlation between length of time in the UK and language ability. (PSI, 1984 p.129). The later ALBSU/RRL survey suggests that the position had improved somewhat by 1989 – 27% of the South Asian language speakers interviewed said that they had had some help in improving their English by joining classes or neighbourhood schemes. However, this rate of improvement is unlikely to accelerate without a considerable increase in government expenditure on English language teaching both at work and in participants' own time. In March 1989 the government terminated national funding of over £2 million for the Industrial Language Training Scheme, resulting in closure of many local ILT Units which were unable to obtain alternative finance. The outlook for language teaching at work looked bleak, and ALBSU emphasized that current provision of English for speakers of other languages was meeting only the tip of the iceberg of estimated need, with less than one in ten of those in need receiving tuition at any one time.

In addition, as those in linguistic minority communities who were born abroad get older, they are likely to lose both the incentive and, in some cases, the ability to learn English. Both the PSI and the LMP surveys found a strong correlation between age and proficiency in English, and this was confirmed by the findings of the 1989 survey by ALBSU, which are set out below:

Table 2.4 Survey 1989

Age	Speaking little or no English (%)	Understanding little or no English (%) Asian Adults
19–25	10	9
26–35	30	28
36–45	31	29
46–55	36	30
56+	46	44

Social Services Departments and Health Authorities are now beginning to respond to the fact that many ethnic minority people now approaching pension age will not retire to their countries of origin. By the time they reach pension age they will have put in twenty, thirty or more years of work in this country and will have put down roots in their communities here through their children and grandchildren and/or social and community links. With little opportunity to learn English while working and perhaps living in an area where shopping and social life could be carried out in their parent-tongue, they are likely to need to communicate through an interpreter if they have to request assistance from public services. It is worth noting that women, with their longer life expectancy, are more likely to need long term residential care, and it is women who are more likely to have difficulty with English.

Factors Affecting Language Acquisition

The effective learning of language depends on a wide range of factors. Some, such as age, educational background and the motivation and opportunity to learn have already been touched on in this chapter. An examination of data from the Linguistic Minorities Project report (see Table 2.5) suggests further factors which may determine whether and how well a person learns English, and indicates the complexity of the processes at work here.

It is often suggested that 'residential concentrations' of members of the same minority group can have the effect of reducing both the need and the motivation to learn English. While the results of the PSI study did in fact suggest this, it is unsafe to assume that the converse will be true – that is, that a residentially dispersed group will, by definition, speak better English.

The Ukrainians, for instance, have adopted a fairly dispersed pattern of settlement in the East Midlands and North of England, yet 50% of those interviewed by LMP said they understood and spoke English 'not very well' or 'not at all'. The bulk of Ukrainians came as refugees or through the European Voluntary Workers scheme in the early fifties. But, here again, length of stay in the UK does not appear to have made a significant difference to levels of English. The main influencing factors appear to have been educational background and economic opportunity. In contrast to the Poles, who represented a broader spread of classes and occupations, many Ukrainians came from rural backgrounds with limited educational possibilities. The conditions of entry as European Voluntary Workers limited the kind of employment that could be undertaken at least for three years after arrival. For men it was agriculture (45%), coal-mining (17%) and domestic service (6%), for women domestic service (40%) and the textile industry (42%) (LMP, 1985 p.77). The majority of the Linguistic Minorities Project's Ukrainian respondents in 1981 were employed in manufacturing industry, 22% working more than forty hours per week. (LMP, p.203).

Long working hours also characterised the Portuguese community (a third were working over 40 hours) and here again the main factor determining low levels of English appears to have been economic. In contrast with the Ukrainians, the majority of Portuguese families came to the UK in the 1960s, to work in hotel and catering industries and in hospital and domestic jobs. Since workers in the hotel and catering industry only had an average weekly wage of around £70 in 1980, they were often forced to find additional employment on a shift-work basis

Table 2.5 Spoken Communication

(Data extracted from the Linguistic Minorities Project Adult Language Use Survey

Respondents Nationality and Location	Respondents understanding and speaking English 'not very well' or 'not at all'	Respondents using only or mostly the minority language at home	Working respondents where all fellow workers can speak the minority language
	%	%	%
Bengali* Coventry London	48 53	64 88	18 39
Chinese** Coventry Bradford London	56 90 53	57 85 73	72 – 64
Greek London	28	51	26
Gujarati*** Coventry London	26 24	67 66	9 21
Italian Coventry London	17 35	21 34	6 28
Panjabi (G)**** Coventry Bradford	33 46	67 76	16 33
Panjabi (U)***** Coventry Bradford	39 64	74 82	16 42
Polish Coventry Bradford	9 16	36 41	2 7
Portuguese London	50	67	12
Turkish London	25	60	22
Ukrainian Coventry	50	63	3

*   *Bengali* includes Sylheti
**   *Chinese* is used as a general heading for a number of languages including Cantonese, Hakka, Vietnamese. (The Bradford sample consisted entirely of recently arrived Vietnamese refugees).
***   *Gujarati* includes Kutchi.

32

Table 2.5 Spoken Communication (cont'd)
(Data extracted from the Linguistic Minorities Project Adult Language Use Survey

Respondents Nationality and Location	Working respondents (who work for someone else) where the boss can speak the minority language	Working respondents where at least one fellow worker can speak the minority language	Working respondents who use only or mostly English with workmates
	%	%	%
Bengali[*] Coventry London	20 32	34 79	53 18
Chinese[**] Coventry Bradford London	– – 53	76 – 81	16 – 18
Greek London	51	66	37
Gujarati[***] Coventry London	2 2	39 69	57 32
Italian Coventry London	3 31	43 65	61 42
Panjabi (G)[****] Coventry Bradford	10 8	72 80	29 24
Panjabi (U)[*****] Coventry Bradford	2 11	68 84	39 9
Polish Coventry Bradford	1 8	47 48	62 65
Portuguese London	5	56	32
Turkish London	31	58	40
Ukrainian Coventry	0	31	69

Notes (cont'd)
****   Panjabi (G) refers to Sikhs, who generally use the Gurmukhi script.
*****   Panjabi (U) refers to Muslims from Pakistan where Urdu is generally the language of literacy. This heading includes Mirpuri.

to supplement their income. This left little time for meeting people outside their own community or for learning English outside the workplace. (LMP, p.61).

It is interesting that the Turkish, Greek and Italian communities were also recorded as working long hours (around 40% worked over forty hours per week) and yet this does not appear to have had the same drastic effect on their ability to learn English. The explanation lies perhaps in the fact that a high proportion of these respondents were self-employed or working in the family business. (LMP, p.203). This may have allowed them greater flexibility to attend classes and perhaps provided a greater incentive through the desire and the need to communicate with English customers in order to enhance the business.

The fact that a high proportion of Panjabis in Bradford were also working in the family business yet nearly half spoke English 'not very well' or 'not at all' may be an indication either of large numbers of customers speaking the same language as the entrepreneur, (a function of the more concentrated settlement pattern) or of greater economic pressures on the Panjabi trader (56% of Bradford Panjabis were recorded as working more than forty hours per week).

The position of the survey's Chinese respondents in London and Coventry gives a clear indication that while self-employment or work in the family business may in certain circumstances assist language acquisition, this is not always the case. Roughly two-thirds of all Chinese-speaking workers in Coventry and London worked in situations where *all* their fellow workers could speak the minority language (Hakka or Cantonese) (LMP, p.206). In small family businesses specialising in Chinese food, contact with customers may be limited to the one family member with some English, the rest of the family working 'back of house'. Opportunities to learn or practice English may therefore be strictly limited.

It is the lack of opportunity to use English at work or outside the home which seems to be the main inhibiting factor for adults rather than the extent to which the minority language is used between family members. The figures given in the table demonstrate that there is no direct relationship between the latter and the ability to speak or understand English. For instance 41% of Polish respondents in Bradford said they used only or mostly Polish at home, but only 16% had difficulties with English. Over two thirds of Gujarati people in London spoke only or mostly Gujarati at home, but only a quarter said they had any difficulties with English. Clearly the main motivator to learn English has to be a desire or need to communicate with English people and this will occur, by definition, mostly outside the home. English may be encountered within the home when children born here begin to see it as their main language and return from school speaking the language of the classroom to their parents. But at this point the latters' motivation is likely to be primarily to encourage the children to speak the minority language to them, so as to keep their language and its associated culture alive. Over 90% of Asian men and women interviewed by PSI agreed with the statement 'it is a good thing to be able to speak the language of your family's area of origin' and nearly as many agreed with a second statement: 'children should be taught the language of their family's country of origin.' The motivation to maintain the parent-tongue is likely to become stronger as the children get older, and if the parents' contact with white English-speakers outside the home is limited, non-existent or acquires negative connotations as a result of unpleasant experiences then there may be a corresponding fall in the motivation to learn English. This may be one of the factors detrmining the correlation between age and lower proficiency in English identified by PSI.

The prognosis in respect of opportunities to use English at work is not good. Employers' recruitment policies over the last twenty years have tended to exclude ethnic minority people from some workplaces and concentrate them in others. For much of the eighties, the economic situation has had the effect of discouraging manual workers from changing jobs because of anxieties about possible redundancy and loss of compensation entitlement. The result is that those minority workers who are able to retain their jobs are likely to continue to work in places where the need to communicate in English is limited. The other side of the coin is that minority workers are more likely to be made redundant because of the high proportion employed in traditional labour-intensive manufacturing industry which is increasingly subject to rationalisation. Those who become redundant and who have limited spoken and written English will be among those who have most difficulty finding other work and who are most vulnerable to racial discrimination by employers. An increasing proportion of this group are likely to become clients of the public services, and probably of Social Services departments in particular as a result of the stress of long-term unemployment.

Ability to Read and Write English: the National Picture

ALBSU's 1989 survey produced the following results shown in Table 2.6.

Table 2.6

Ability level (self-assessed)	Reading %	Writing %
Not at all	17	20
A little	19	20
Fairly well	16	15
Very well	30	27
Excellently	19	18

Source: ALBSU/RRL, 1989 p. 10.

As with speaking and understanding English, men were able to read and write English, in general, better than women, and the proportions reading or writing English a little or not at all increased with age.

The existence of substantial groups of people who read and write English to only a limited extent, or not at all, has serious implications, considering how far the ability to get work, participate in democratic processes and obtain service in Britain depends on an ability to deal with the written word. It suggests considerable dependency on family and friends for translation of letters from public bodies – where such assistance is available. It is undoubtedly a factor in the low take-up of certain benefits and services by members of ethnic minority groups (see *Communication Ability and Disadvantage* below).

Although the language groupings used in the ALBSU/RRL survey do not coincide exactly with those in the earlier LMP study, there are striking simularities in the results, which suggest that little progress has been made, over the last decade, in meeting the need to improve reading and writing among speakers of English as a second language. This may well stem from a preoccupation with 'improving spoken English before trying to tackle reading and writing.' Whatever the explanation, the figures given in Table 2.7 are very similar to those given for similar groups in the 1989 study, and this must give cause for concern.

On the other hand, both studies also found that the majority (four out of five in the more recent ALBSU/RRL report) *were* literate to some degree in their first language. Table 2.7 shows that, with the exception of Panjabi and Bengali-speakers, the proportion of those who were unable to read and write in either English or their first language was found by LMP to be very small. This suggests that leaflets and publicity in ethnic minority languages are likely to be very worthwhile as a means of reaching people who otherwise receive information second-hand or not at all. Bilingual information (*eg.* a leaflet printed in English on one side and in the minority language on the other) is likely to be the most effective, as people with different levels of competence in the two languages will be able to use the one to help the other.

It is sometimes suggested that producing leaflets in minority languages reinforces feelings of inadequacy among speakers of these languages who are illiterate in their own language.

The small numbers involved do not suggest that this is a valid reason for not printing publicity in minority languages. It is also important to remember that such publicity signals acceptance of the different language and culture of minority groups – even to those who cannot read it – and that an illiterate person will probably prefer to have a relative read the leaflet out in their own language, rather than have the relative translate an English version. From the point of view of the agency producing the publicity, there is always a risk of mistranslation when relying on relatives to translate. This risk is eliminated if the literate relative has a minority language version to read direct to the illiterate recipient.

Table 2.7 Written Communication

Respondents Nationality and location	Respondents reading/writing English 'not very well' or 'not at all'	Respondents unable to read/ write in English or in the minority language
	%	%
Bengali		
Coventry	63	10
London	60	9
Chinese		
Coventry	70	2
Bradford	94	6
London	58	2
Greek		
London	43	3
Gujarati		
Coventry	36	2
London	28	1
Italian		
Coventry	61	1
London	66	0
Panjabi (G)		
Coventry	40	8
Bradford	55	18
Panjabi (U)		
Coventry	56	27
Bradford	72	29
Polish		
Coventry	36	0
Bradford	45	0
Portuguese		
London	73	4
Turkish		
London	54	3
Ukrainian		
Coventry	69	0

See LMP, 1985 Tables 5.2 P. 188 and 5.4 P. 193.

*   *Bengali* includes Sylheti
**   *Chinese* is used as a general heading for a number of languages including Cantonese, Hakka, Vietnamese. (The Bradford sample consisted entirely of recently arrived Vietnamese refugees).
***   *Gujarati* includes Kutchi.
****   Panjabi (G) refers to Sikhs, who generally use the Gurmukhi script.
*****   Panjabi (U) refers to Muslims from Pakistan where Urdu is generally the language of literacy. This heading includes Mirpuri.

Communication Ability and Disadvantage

There are clear links between the ability to communicate effectively in English and various forms of social disadvantage. Connections with unemployment and ageing have already been made. Here we focus on other aspects of disadvantage which suggest that a higher proportion of Asians and other ethnic minority people with limited English are likely to be potential or actual clients of Social Services departments and other helping organisations.

Job Levels

It was to be expected that PSI would find a strong relationship between fluency in English and job levels. 21% of Asian men fluent in English were found to be in semi-skilled or unskilled manual jobs, compared with 70% of men who spoke English slightly or not at all; the corresponding figures for women were 24% and 87% (PSI, p.158 and Table 94). Employees in jobs of this kind are more likely to have low earnings and are also more vulnerable to redundancy.

Housing Deprivation

Less obvious was the PSI finding that the proportion of Asian households lacking exclusive use of basic amenities was twice as high for household heads with limited English as it was for those with fluent English (PSI, Table 68).

Not only does restricted communication ability mean poor job prospects, lower income and therefore lower purchasing power when it comes to raising a mortgage or paying rent, but it probably also means limited' choice in terms of ability to use the various channels for obtaining housing. Whether this means using estate agents, local newspaper advertisements, Council housing department, the ability to read, fill in forms, use the telephone and to negotiate are essential. Once in sub-standard housing, the various ways of getting improvements made – either through the landlord, through the environmental health officer, or, in the case of owner-occupiers, through an improvement grant, once again depend on good communication and negotiation.

The situation is all the more stark when one considers that between 1974 and 1981 the housing conditions of black people in general improved. The proportion of black people without sole use of bath, hot water or inside WC fell from 37% to 7% (in comparison with a fall among whites from 18% to 5%).

Significantly, PSI noted that the overall gap between whites and blacks was now located in the Asian sample, as the proportion of West Indians lacking or sharing these facilities were the same as for whites (PSI, p.94).

Ironically, Asians with limited English living in poor housing conditions were also more likely to be adversely affected by the change from the rates to the community charge system in 1990. A survey undertaken in London showed that 13.1% of Asians lived in households with more than three adults, in contrast with 10% of Afro-Caribbeans and 4.6% of whites (ALA, 1988).

Asians with limited English were more likely to have adopted extended family living arrangements for mutual support, and were therefore likely to pay more under the new system – even though they were as we have seen, probably living in inferior housing conditions.'

Low Take-up of Benefits and Services

In the light of the links made so far between limited English and low income, unemployment and poor housing, it is cause for concern that there are strong indications of a link between communication difficulties and low take-up of benefits and services.

For instance, a research project on benefit take-up among claimants in general in the London Borough of Islington in 1984 found that the Bengali and Greek-Cypriot respondents were particularly likely to be underclaiming.

The Bengali-speaking people interviewed had low levels of English and were often confused by the information available on benefits and wary of approaching the local authority and the DHSS for advice. Many lived in bad housing on an estate where the National Front was active and the researchers reported a strong degree of suspicion of outsiders.

Many of those contacted lived in old, damp and bitterly cold flats:

'There were no fires installed with the tenancy and few could afford to buy and install gas fires for themselves. Those that had heating had one/two bar electric fires. The households in receipt of supplementary benefit had not known prior to the contact made by the project that they could claim a single payment for heating appliances and when told about the entitlement were reluctant to claim . . .' (IPR, p.6).

Some of this reluctance was found to be rooted in insecurities about their right to stay in Britain:

'Fears were expressed of the consequences of claiming anything which might bring attention to them and cause 'trouble'. Even though everyone we made contact with seemed to be in England legally and to have full rights to claim, there was fear that their right stay could be affected by claiming. This fear must have been heightened by their isolation in a white and, to varying degrees, hostile community.' (IPR, p.5).

Whereas the previous work of the project had found that most people were claiming the 'basic' benefits of child benefit and supplementary benefit this could not be assumed with the Bengali-speaking community. People contacted were unfamiliar with the benefit system generally, and this included child benefit. Similar evidence was presented to the Home Affairs Committee during its study of the Bangladeshi community, and the Committee expressed a wish 'to see more interpreters employed in areas with substantial numbers of Bangladeshis, and would ultimately expect to see Bangladeshis adequately represented among social security staff in those areas' (HAC, 1986, para. 83). The isolation of the comparatively small Bengali-speaking community in Islington appears to have made the problem more acute, but underclaiming also occurs in larger ethnic minority communities. For instance, a take-up campaign in Sandwell, West Midlands where 11.4% of the population is black, resulted in £173,387 in additional (annual) benefits for ethnic minority claimants (CPAG, 1985 p.85).

The ability to cope with the written word is an essential pre-requisite for anyone wanting to handle their own social security claim effectively. In addition to its Bengali-speaking respondents, the Islington survey checked the welfare benefit entitlement of thirty Greek-Cypriot elderly. Twenty-one were found not to be claiming all the benefits to which they were entitled.

> 'The lack of ability to read English or distinguish various types of letters was evident. When the project made contact with a claimant at home or in the group they would produce mounds of correspondence of all kinds, from LEB bills, to DHSS letters, to advertisements offering 4p off washing-up liquid. All were indistinguishable to them and had relatively the same status. Talking through their history of claiming the impression was one of taking pot-luck with claiming and whether they were receiving the correct amounts or not. With no direct facilities available either at DHSS or at the local authority they have limited means of negotiating the benefit system or knowing their correct entitlement. They made little distinction between the various statutory authorities, for example DHSS and local Council. Trying to explain the then newly introduced housing benefit scheme through a translator was extremely difficult.' (IPR p.11).

There are some indications of a link between take-up and language in relation to disability. Horn's survey of referrals of Asian families to four Social Services Area offices in Bradford (NISW, 1982) reports that most of the twenty-one applications relating to disabled people asked for 'fairly specific help; where they did not, it was because the family did not speak sufficient English and was not aware that any help with aids was available'.

These families seemed to have passively accepted their child's disability and it was difficult to get over to them that aids and services were designed to maximise their child's potential. An interpreter remarked that it was also extremely difficult to translate this idea without implying that aids were something which would help the child 'get better'.

> 'The consequences of these families' lack of knowledge were seen in the case of a 20-year-old girl with muscular dystrophy where it took

the social worker weeks of patient encouragement to get her to accept that she could go out in a wheelchair and have a measure of independence from her mother, where previously the girl had completely accepted her own helplessness. This girl was actually referred by the home tutor who came to teach her and her mother English . . . This situation suggests that while the health service may now be picking up Asian children disabled at birth or in infancy, there may still be older disabled Asians who are unknown because they rarely go out, and who need social work help.' (Horn, p.66).

Overall, the coincidence of employment, income and housing disadvantage, already mentioned, with limited ability to speak English, and the studies of Social Security underclaiming among this group, all suggest that take-up of Social Services support is also likely to be disproportionately low.

The availability of interpreters should play an important role in making services more accessible and user-friendly to clients with limited English.

The National Picture: Conclusions

There is clear evidence of a continuing need for interpreting provision among a substantial proportion of the ethnic minority community whose first language is not English.

Although the levels of English spoken by members of Britain's Asian communities have, on average, been improving, the rate of improvement has been slow. Apart from factors such as socio-economic background, education and status in the country of origin, this is primarily due to two factors which are unlikely to change significantly in the near future without positive action at government level firstly, the under-resourcing of language teaching for adults, particularly in the workplace, and, secondly, the constraints imposed on many ethnic minority people by their position in the labour market.

The experience of racism is also likely to have reduced the motivation of some people to learn English. The surveys quoted in this chapter have identified a substantial proportion of the population who are likely to need, and continue to need, interpreters.

The presence of an increasing number of ethnic minority elderly, and the effect of changes in the labour market situation both mean that public services are likely to experience a growing need for interpreting provision. This conclusion is supported by the evidence linking limited English with other forms of disadvantage in housing and take-up of Social Security benefits. There is some evidence that Asians do not make sufficient use of services specifically offered by Social Services departments, and this seems likely in the light of the general link between limited English and disadvantage. An increasing number of Social Services departments are now monitoring the ethnic origin of clients and it is to be hoped that this will provide opportunities for further research in this area.

Exploring Local Needs for Interpreting Provision

Local authorities considering the need for interpreting provision – particularly when preparing a possible Section 11 application – usually begin with census information about ethnic minority residents. While this provides basic data about countries of origin, age, housing, areas of residence and economic activity, it gives no information on language or communication ability. Where the local authority has carried out a survey of languages spoken at home by pupils in its schools – or where similar information can be extracted from primary school application data – this can be a useful guide to the extent of bilingualism in the area. Again, however, it does not establish the extent of the need for interpreting provision.

Sessional Interpreting as a Source of Data

Where the authorities already use sessional interpreters sufficiently often, the most economical – and also the most practically useful – way of establishing the extent of need is to monitor this service. Account will need to be taken of the extent to which it is publicised and available, so that any gap between supply and demand can be estimated. As already noted, bilingual staff often help out as interpreters and this is rarely recorded. It will be important for any such monitoring exercise to include them.

Where a sessional register does not exist, but there is a prima facie need for interpreting, the authority may decide to fund a pilot sessional service with a co-ordinator/outreach worker to recruit interpreters, link them with users and monitor usage. Monitoring should include, at least, the following: numbers of clients requesting an interpreter; numbers of staff requesting an interpreter; numbers of requests met; languages required; types of case involved; average length of sessions with same client; numbers of sessions with same client; origins of requests within the authority; geographical distribution of requests from clients/community organisations; and differentiation between interpreting and translation.

Even if the exercise does not produce evidence to justify the need for a permanent interpreter, it will produce a register of sessional interpreters who can be called on in the future!

Staff Surveys

Another way of building up data from internal sources is to conduct a staff survey drawing on the experience of both black and white employees dealing with the public. Two examples of this approach are given below.

The Leeds Survey

In October 1987 Leeds Social Services department undertook an investigation into communication difficulties between fieldwork staff and ethnic minority clients. Forms were completed for four hundred and twenty-nine of the latter by one hundred and five social workers/ social welfare officers and specialist staff.

The survey results were computerised and enabled the department to establish inter alia: allocation patterns by ethnic origin of client and of social worker; geographical distribution of clients; mother tongue of client; age pattern of clients by ethnic origin; case details; communication difficulties and steps taken by staff to overcome them.

The survey came to the following conclusions:

'1) Interpreting skills are being sought by staff to assist their communication with clients, and a policy needs to be determined on the use of interpreters within the department.

2) Minority ethnic staff contribute in significant ways to the overall service provided to minority ethnic clients: a clearer definition of the different tasks that need to be performed by minority ethnic staff is required, and the implications for future development in staffing and grading of different posts, training and qualifications need to be considered.

3) A range of training issues should be considered to assist both white and minority ethnic staff in their work with minority ethnic clients. Sources of advice and consultancy might also be investigated.'

(Leeds, 1988)

This survey relied on members of staff's own perceptions of their own ability to communicate with clients. While it is important to establish this, our experience is that white mono-lingual staff frequently overrate their ability to communicate with people who have limited English. They are often also unaware of the extent to which clients do not take the initiative in interaction because of their English. A training exercise designed by one of the authors to investigate this found that even Asian participants who were quite fluent in English often felt that they could only partially express their personality in interaction with English people, when compared to interaction in their own first language. Unfortunately, there is no statistical basis for correcting for white respondents over-rating their own ability to communicate – but it should be borne in mind when interpreting results.

The Hertfordshire Survey

A questionnaire was sent to all social work teams, home care officers, divisional occupational therapists, specialist teams, residential establishments and day centres, asking about: the number of clients known; their country of origin, religion and language; whether or not they spoke English.

A disturbing finding from this survey was that of clients who did not speak English, nearly one third fell into the 'children at risk category'.

The report pointed to 'a pressing and immediate' need for social services staff in direct contact with clients from ethnic minority groups to have a clearly identifiable means of access to interpreting services. 'Difficulties arise at present, for example, when children sometimes as young as ten, have to act as interpreter between their parents and a social worker. This not only places the burden of such a complex task on a young person, but also leads to misunderstandings of where the problems in the family may lie and what can be done to help'. (Herts, 1986).

Consultation with Ethnic Minority Groups and Voluntary Organisations in the Community

Community groups usually have extensive experience of language difficulties and interpreting. Prior to setting up its joint local authority/ health authority interpreting project, London Borough of Greenwich collected evidence of need from a variety of groups. Examples included:

1) *Greenwich Council for Racial Equality*
   Worker with Asian elderly spent about fifteen hours per week interpreting at hospitals
2) *Age Concern Greenwich*
   A volunteer Asian worker interpreted at hospitals about four times per week
3) *The Vietnamese Refugee Project*
   One member of staff was fully engaged in interpreting, most of this at hospitals. They could only afford to send an interpreter for a first appointment or when an interpreter was acutely needed. Other requests were turned down.
4) *Greenwich MIND*
   The Asian Research Worker interviewed 30 Asian women – twenty-two said they would need an interpreter to communicate with the authorities
5) *North Charlton Community Project*
   Part-time Asian Advice Worker received ten to fifteen requests per week to interpret. She could only respond to a few of these requests and advised the remainder how to tackle the interview themselves. However, these clients usually reported that they had received a poor service as a result of not having an interpreter.

This kind of consultation is particularly important in the case of Section 11 applications, given the Home Office requirement that appropriate consultation with representatives of recipients of the special service to be provided should have taken place.

LARRIE

The Local Authorities Race Relations Exchange houses a growing number of local authority documents on race equality from all over Britain. This includes budgets, strategy papers, staffing arrangements and job descriptions from local authorities who have already considered the issue of interpreting. A scan of the catalogue of documents

nicate in English equally to all racial groups using its services could be discriminating, because a considerably smaller proportion of black linguistic minority groups would be able to comply with it. The risk of such discrimination is substantially increased, when the authority has an actual – or implied – legal duty to communicate effectively with members of the public.

In this chapter we examine the communication and interpreting implications of the main statutory provisions in respect of children, mentally ill people, sick and disabled people as well as housing legislation and general provisions affecting the courts and the police. Although the general duty to eliminate unlawful discrimination and promote equal opportunity set out in Section 71 of the Race Relations Act applies to local authorities only, it is important to note that Section 20 (see below) applies to the provision of goods, facilities or services *by any public authority or profession*.

Relevant Provisions of the Race Relations Act 1976

Section 71

This section imposes a duty on all local authorities to make appropriate arrangements with a view to securing that their various functions are carried out with due regard to the need to eliminate unlawful discrimination, and to promote equality of opportunity and good relations between persons of different racial groups.

Section 20

This section makes it unlawful for anyone who is concerned with the provision of goods, facilities or services to discriminate by refusing or deliberately omitting to provide them or, as regards their quality or the manner or the terms on which s/he provides them.

Discrimination of this kind is unlawful irrespective of whether the goods, facilities or services are provided for payment or free of charge. The Act specifies the services of any profession or trade or any local or public authority as being within the purview of this section.

Legislation in Respect of Children

Children Act 1989

The duty placed on local authorities to investigate where they have 'reasonable cause to suspect that a child is suffering or is likely to suffer significant harm' clearly implies an ability to communicate adequately, and the importance of accurate assessment is underlined by the provisions for child assessment orders and emergency protection orders.

A court may only make a care or supervision order if it is satisfied on the 'significant harm' criterion, and section 31 specifies that the harm, or likelihood of harm, must be attributable to:

'(i) the care given to the child, or likely to be given to him if the order were not made, not being what it would be reasonable to expect a parent to give to him; or
(ii) the child being beyond parental control'

The wording of the Act leaves a considerable amount to the interpretation of the courts, and raises interesting issues relating to cultural differences in the definition of what it would be reasonable to expect of a parent.

Section 22 sets out the duties of local authorities in relation to children looked after by them. Before making any decision about such a child, the local authority must 'as far as is reasonably practical' ascertain the wishes and feelings of the child, his parents and other relevant persons specified in the Act. They must also give due consideration to 'the child's religious persuasion, racial origin and cultural and linguistic background.'

These and other decisions about the welfare of children covered by the Act clearly imply that where either the child or relevant family members speak little or no English, an interpreter should be used in order to comply with the intention of the law.

Adoption Act 1976

Consents to adoption: an order cannot be made unless the court is satisfied that each parent or guardian 'freely, and with full understanding of what is involved, agrees unconditionally'. It is a very serious matter for the court to dispense with the consent of the parent or guardian, and adequate communication with all relevant individuals is essential, before a report and recommendation are presented in court.

Any wishes of the parents or guardians as to the religious upbringing of the child must be taken into account.

Courts must give first consideration to the welfare of the child 'and shall so far as practicable ascertain the wishes and feelings of the child regarding the decision . . . having regard to his age and understanding.' Where a child does not speak fluent English, 'so far as practicable' implies the use of an interpreter.

Legislation Relating to Mentally Ill People

Compulsory admission procedures under the Mental Health Act 1983 include a duty to inform the nearest relative of the patient, and may therefore require an interpreter. The same applies to the right of the nearest relative to be consulted where an approved social worker is considering an application for treatment or guardianship, and to the right to be informed of the patient's imminent discharge 'if practicable . . . at least 7 days before the date of discharge'. (Although the responsibility for information re discharge rests with the hospital authorities, in practice a social worker is likely to be involved).

Before making an application for admission, the approved social worker must 'satisfy himself that detention in hospital is in all the circumstances of the case the most appropriate way of providing the care and medical treatment of which the patient stands in need'. This part of the Act (s13) goes on to specify that 'an approved social worker shall interview the patient in a suitable manner' before making any application and in this respect the DHSS have drawn attention to the need to take account of 'any hearing or linguistic difficulties the patient may have'. (Explanatory Memorandum) Another writer comments that 'the social worker must be prepared for people who speak a different language, or who are deaf or who present some other communication difficulty. Approved social workers should know how to contact interpreters'. (Brown, 1983)

The Social Services Department has a duty to provide a social report on the patient 'as soon as practicable' after admission. This should include 'the past history of the patient's mental disorder, his present condition and the social, familial and personal factors bearing on it'. In a situation where English is not the first language of the patient or other relevant individuals, an interpreter will be essential.

The same applies to the responsibility for providing reports for mental health review tribunals. These should include 'full information about the patient's home situation, employment and housing prospects in the area to which he might be discharged, his nearest relative's attitude, and the availability of medical facilities and community support. (BASW, 1983)

Similar considerations will apply to the patient's right to statutory aftercare (s117) 'until such time as the DHA and the local social services authority are satisfied that the person concerned is no longer in need of such services'. Accurate assessment naturally depends on effective communication.

Under s132 the hospital managers are required to inform a detained patient, both verbally and in writing:

1) Under which provision of the Act s/he is being detained.
2) His/her rights to apply to a Mental Health Review Tribunal.
3) His/her rights regarding consent to treatment.
4) His/her rights to receive post, and the limitation of this.

The hospital managers are required to ensure that the patient *understands* these rights as far as is practicable.

Legislation Relating to Sick and Disabled People

Chronically Sick and Disabled Persons Act 1970

Apart from the local authority's general duty to determine need and supply information on a broad scale, the mandatory duty to provide practical assistance in the home where need is established implies effective assessment which cannot take place if communication is inadequate. The same applies to the provision of Home Helps under the National Health Services Act 1977.

Disabled Persons (Services, Consultation and Representation) Act 1986

Section 3 of this Act requires the local authority to allow disabled persons to make representations as to their needs before they make their assessment. Where English is not the disabled person's first language, an interpreter will be needed. The 'authorised representatives' provided for under Section 1 and 2 of the Act may include interpreters.

National Assistance Act 1948

Section 47 of this Act empowers the local authority to remove chronically sick, aged, or physically incapacitated people from their homes, where they are unable to devote to themselves, and are not receiving from anyone else, proper care and attention. This removal can be compulsory, and seven days notice must be given to the patient of the local authority's intention to apply to a magistrate for an order.

Six weeks after such an order has been made, and the person concerned has been removed to a suitable hospital 'or other place within convenient distance of the area of the authority', the person removed – or someone acting on his or her behalf – can apply for the order to be revoked. Effective communication will clearly be important in both the assessment and in terms of the exercise of the client's rights. In particular, it will be important for the social worker to ensure that limited English is not mistaken for confusion in elderly people.

Housing Legislation

Housing Act 1985

The definition of whether or not a person or family are homeless in the terms of the Act may involve assessment of complicated accommodation arrangements and family relationships. The accuracy of establishing whether or not someone is intentionally homeless – and therefore not entitled to assistance from the LA housing service – clearly depends on effective communication. Given that families with children who are deemed intentionally homeless may need help from the social services department under S1 of the Child Care Act 1980, a social worker involved may want to call on the services of an interpreter as early as possible in the assessment process.

General Provisions *re* the Courts and the Police

It is a fundamental principle of both civil and criminal justice in Britain that parties to the proceedings should be able to understand what is going on.

The United Kingdom is a signatory to the *European Convention on Human Rights and Fundamental Freedoms (1953)* which provides that everyone charged with a criminal offence has certain basic rights, including: 'to be informed promptly, in a language which he understands and in detail, of the nature and cause of the accusation against him; and to have the free assistance of an interpreter if he cannot understnd or speak the language used in court'.

These rights have been built into subsequent UK legislation, not only in relation to the Welsh linguistic minority but also in relation to anyone whose first language is not English. (The Welsh Language Act 1967 gives the parties in legal proceedings the right to speak Welsh and places a duty on the court to provide an interpreter.)

Criminal Cases

Section 17 of the Administration of Justice Act 1973 placed a duty on criminal courts to pay for an interpreter where a defendant lacks English. The court may order an interpreter to be provided, even where the defendant does not request one, if the judge believes this to be necessary. (R. V. Lee Kun, (1916) lk.b 337)

In cases where a prosecution witness lacks English and an interpreter is required – or where an interpreter is required to give evidence for the prosecution regarding previous interpreting work, payment is made by:

1) The court in all indictable cases.
2) The police in all summary cases or appeals arising from summary cases.

If an interpreter is required to attend court in any case prosecuted by police or the Crown where a defence witness lacks English, payment of the fee is the responsibility of the defence.

Civil Cases

In civil cases, the court has the discretion to pay an interpreter the same rate as a witness of fact – or, if the judge or registrar thinks fit – 'such sum as might be allowed if he had attended court as an expert witness'. (Order 47, Rule 34A, County Court Rules 1936).

Where plaintiff or defendant are entitled to Legal Aid an interpreter's services can usually be paid for from the Legal Aid Fund.

In case of Kashich v. Kashich (1951) an order for maintenance in favour of the wife was set aside on appeal to the Divisional Court on the grounds that the husband, who had been represented and had not had any interpreter, could not, in the court's view, have fully understood what was going on. It should not normally be difficult to persuade a judge that provision of an interpreter is the best way to ensure that the proceedings are not queried later.

Police Procedures

Police procedures are given in the Police and Criminal Evidence Act 1984, and in the Code of Practice issued under the Act.

'A person must not be interviewed in the absence of a person capable of acting as interpreter, if:

(a) he has difficulty in understanding English;

(b) the interviewing officer cannot himself speak the person's language; and

(c) the person wishes an interpreter to be present.'

This rule can only be waived by an officer of the rank of superinten-
dent or above, if he or she considers that delay will involve an
immediate risk of harm to persons or serious loss of or serious
damage to property. (Code C. Annex C).'

The Code also gives detailed guidance on the taking of statements
through an interpreter.

'The interviewing officer shall ensure that the interpreter makes a
note of the interview at the time in the language of the person being
interviewed for use in the event of his being called to give evidence,
and certifies its accuracy. The person shall be given an opportunity
to read it or have it read to him and sign it as correct or to indicate
the respects in which he considers it inaccurate. If the interview is
tape-recorded the arrangements set out in the relevant code of
practice apply.' (Code para. 14.2).

In the case of a person making a statement in a language other than
English:

(a) the interpreter shall take down the statement in the language in
which it is made;

(b) the person making the statement shall be invited to sign it; and

(c) an official English translation shall be made in due course. (Code
para. 14.3).

The responsibility for obtaining the services of an interpreter in such
circumstances rests with the police. While this is, generally in the
interest of the member of the public concerned, there can be problems – for instance if the defence solicitor wishes to take further and
urgent instructions from his or her client in a private. Where the
interpreter has been 'instructed' by the police it may be considered
inappropriate for the latter to participate in private interview between
defence solicitor and client.

The Law Society wrote to us that they 'would very much like there to
be a reliable pool of accredited interpreters available for use by the
defence – to save reliance on the police interpreters – and for there to
be some assurance that their costs would be paid.' At present the legal
aid authorities can pay for an interpreter as a disbursement 'actually
and reasonably incurred' under the remuneration regulations. This
payment may, however, have to be justified and may not be regarded
as reasonable if the prosecution have offered an interpreter. In practice,
therefore, many solicitors tend to use the interpreter offered by the
prosecution in order to avoid any difficulty about costs.

The need for a panel of interpreters available other than via the police or prosecution is reinforced by the following observation made to us by Legal Aid Head Office:

> 'Our staff find that while interpreters are widely used at courts and in police stations, there are very few claims for the cost of providing an interpreter to sit in on an interview between a client and his or her solicitor in the office. Claims of this sort would very often come within the advice and assistance, known as 'green form' arrangements.'

It seems likely that solicitors are 'getting by' using the language abilities of their staff or their clients' relatives and friends – perhaps because they have no quick and reliable access to community interpreters with the necessary skills.

It may also be, however, that solicitors are themselves unclear about the position regarding payment of interpreters in such situations. At the time of writing, the Law Society had no guidelines on the payment of interpreters.

Conclusions

The decision whether or not to call in an interpreter may have legal implications which affect both the rights of the individual citizen and the ability of the professional involved to deliver a service effectively and fairly. The Race Relations Act 1976 laid the basis for complaints of discrimination against public bodies which fail to provide an interpreter when it would be equitable to do so, and in our opinion it is only a matter of time before such a case is brought. The best 'insurance' against such an eventuality is for public service organisations and professional bodies to develop clear policy and practice on the provision of interpreters, so that their employees and members know exactly where they stand.

Chapter 4

Social Work in Multi-Racial Areas Interpreting Provision as Good Practice

The employment of interpreters as permanent staff in a Social Services Area Office, and the provision of relevant training for both interpreters and the social workers and other staff using their services, can make an important contribution to the ability of the Area Team to provide a service which is:

1) *Accessible*: clients feel equally able to approach staff whatever their ethnic origin or language, and know, as far as is practicable, what services they may be able to obtain.
2) *Relevant*: assistance is appropriately offered or refused, enforcement or sanctions are appropriately applied.
3) *Effective*: casework objectives are achieved.

This chapter explores some of the ways in which interpreters can make this kind of contribution, drawing where appropriate on interviews with social workers carried out by the authors at the Southall office of London Borough of Ealing Social Services department in 1987 and interviews with Asian clients at the same office in the following year.

An Accessible Service

'Ideally, the service itself should be able to meet (the clients) confusion at the door and expect that stress will be not only about the problem in which help is required, but also about the situation encountered in negotiating one's way through the ritual of an office.' (BASW, 1982 p. 43).

A healthy proportion of self-referrals is a sign of an accessible office. If clients are unsure of their ability to communicate in English, they are likely to think twice about approaching the office without a family member or friend to interpret. Sometimes the latter are not available or the person needing help does not dare ask, with the result that the 'client' may never come through the door.

We interviewed a small cross-section of Asian clients (43) at the Southall Area office, to explore use and perceptions of the interpreting service which had been set up three years previously. This consisted of two full-time interpreters based at the office but available to social workers throughout the Ealing department.

Seventeen of those interviewed were first time callers, and a further ten had first become involved with the office less than a month before the interview. Nine others had been in contact with the office for up to a year, and a further seven were long-term clients of more than two years' standing. 75% of the total used an interpreter in their dealings with the department, and several of those who used English said they were not always sure if they understood what was said to them or were getting their point across.

Two of those who were making their first visit to the office had already been in contact with the department – and the interpreter – elsewhere. A further one had been told by the health visitor that an interpreter would be available. Of the fourteen remaining, eight had come to the office alone because they had heard on the 'grapevine' that an interpreter could be requested.

A notice in English and Panjabi had been put on the notice-board next to the reception-desk some three months before the interviews took place, informing clients that they could ask for an interpreter.

It is difficult to assess the impact of the notice. Only nine of the forty-three interviewed said when asked, that they had seen it. Some of those who had not seen it later pointed out that it was not in Urdu or Gujarati and that they would therefore not have been able to read it in any case. However, it is possible that the notice was read by callers who did not themselves need an interpreter, but who then passed the word around. What is definite is that more than half of those who 'referred themselves' to the Southall Office and were interviewed needed help with communication, but had taken the risk of coming without assistance, because they understood an interpreter would be available.

As is usually the case with 'grapevine' information, coverage was patchy. Four of those interviewed said they had called because they knew one of the receptionists was able to speak Panjabi (only one of these was a first time caller). Three (including the latter) did not know the office employed interpreters.

The presence of bilingual staff apart from interpreters is also likely to contribute to the accessibility of an office. Two of those interviewed had Asian social workers – although in one case the Gujarati speaking social worker and Panjabi-speaking client communicated in Hindi as they had no other language in common. However, at the time of the survey Asian bilingual social workers represented as yet only a very small proportion of the total staff.

Thirty of the thirty-two who used an interpreter told the interviewers that they would ask for an interpreter in the future. Of the two others, one preferred to bring her daughter-in-law anyway, for support, and the other said 'it could be that the interpreter is not in the office, so I would bring someone just to be sure.'

This group was also asked to say what they felt the interpreter was there to do, because some social workers had earlier expressed a concern that clients might assume that the Social Services interpreters were there to act as client advocates. In fact, almost all the replies were along the lines of 'to interpret; to explain; to make me (and/or the social workers) understand; to pass messages; to solve the language problem; to communicate for both sides.' Only two people felt the interpreter was there to speak on the client's behalf or 'make sure that help was given'. The balance changed slightly in reply to a follow-up question ('was the interpreter on your side, the departments' side or neutral?) Four clients felt the Social Services interpreter was on the client's side, and a further three who had used family members to interpret also felt this. However, this needs to be set against the twenty-five who felt the interpreter was neutral and did not take sides.

In general, clients felt that the interpreter had done a good job and was satisfied that good communication had taken place, even though in five cases the clients were not entirely happy with the outcome. In these cases, only one person felt that communication factors had contributed to his dissatisfaction. No Social Services interpreter had been available for this one elderly Panjabi man, and another Panjabi-speaking client in the waiting-room had been asked to interpret for him. This had turned out to be a very frustrating experience for the elderly client, who felt that his points were not being conveyed properly, and that his ad hoc 'interpreter' did not even appear interested. He had in fact intervened in the process of interpreting and tried to get his message over in broken English. Not surprisingly, this client said afterwards that the department should make sure it had qualified interpreters available.

This incident is a good example of the unsatisfactory situation which can arise when an interpreter or bilingual social worker is not available. The elderly client was forced to confide his private business to a complete stranger in whom he rapidly lost confidence. This kind of experience is likely to be passed on down the community 'grapevine' later, and apart from its effect on the client, can do considerable harm to the accessible image the Area Office is trying to build up. Since there will always be some times when interpreters are not available, due to pressure of work, holidays, sickness, emergencies etc., this emphasises the importance of a recuitment strategy which builds up the proportion of Asian bilingual staff, who can step in when such contingencies arise.

Clients were asked, given a choice of interpreter from either their own family, a community organisation or the Social Services department, which one they would prefer. Twenty-nine of the thirty-two who needed an interpreter said they would prefer a Social Services interpreter. The reasons given were, in summary:

1) Friends or family don't have the experience; Social Services interpreters can be trained.
2) You can't always trust friends or family; Social Services interpreters have to respect confidentiality.
3) It's easier for the social worker and department interpreter to co-ordinate appointments.

Professional interpreting, available at the point of contact between the client and the social worker, was seen as a major advantage.

This view was not always shared by the social workers interviewed the previous year. Some had expressed a reluctance to work with the interpreters, for a number of reasons:

"You get a better rapport without an interpreter. I only use one with people who speak no English at all, because it reduces spontaneity."
"The client has a heavy Indian accent and I do find him hard to understand. Sometimes the words get very mixed up, especially when he's upset. But to be upset and cry is sometimes important, and to do this in front of two people can be threatening. It can only happen when a good relationship has been established. I actually think it worked better not using an interpreter."

Clearly, there may be cases when it is better not to use an interpreter, and the social worker must exercise his or her professional judgement in this respect. On the other hand, the comments raise the question of the client's right to ask for an interpreter. The social worker might feel more 'spontaneous' without one but the client might feel more confident with one. Several of the clients interviewed who did not use an interpreter said they were not completely sure of their English, and one who could speak some English asked for an interpreter to be present 'to fill the gaps'. To limit the use of interpreters to those clients who speak no English at all may well deny some clients an important opportunity to communicate. The second comment – 'sometimes the words get mixed up, especially when he's upset' is relevant here. A reduction in communication ability when under stress is a common phenomenon between speakers who share a common language and culture, let alone in situations when the client is speaking a second language. Some clients appreciate the presence of an interpreter simply to help out when they have difficulties. In this case the interpreter's presence guarantees effective communication throughout with a corresponding increase in the client's confidence in the process. Examples given by other social workers included:

1) The client revealed more because someone who shared the same language and culture was present.
2) The client spoke 'enough English to get by, but nothing more complex than that'.
3) The client's own interpreter (a family member) was inappropriate or inadequate (especially where the child kept 'taking over').

4) The social worker knew the client understood some English but wanted to be sure all the information was getting across.
5) The husband understood English, but the wife did not.
6) The client spoke English, but his parents did not.
7) There was a need to deal with difficult feelings and concepts.
8) For the first visit, to ensure that clients understood the social worker's role.
9) The client felt more confident and comfortable with the interpreter present, although she spoke English quite well. The client wanted to be sure she could get everything she wanted across to the social worker.

To sum up, our interviews with clients suggested that the availability of interpreters did make the Area Office more accessible to Asian clients. Most saw the interpreter as a facilitator of communication rather than an advocate and said that they would prefer a Social Services interpreter to either a community or family interpreter. There was some disagreement among social workers about the circumstances in which an interpreter should be used, and we return to this subject (Chapter 6) when discussing the Code of Practice which was subsequently evolved during pilot training courses run for social workers from Southall and other parts of Ealing Social Services department.

Monitoring the demand for and use of the interpreting service and 'market research' among clients to determine the degree of knowledge of services available is essential to the development of accessibility. There is as yet very little research data on the perceptions Asian clients have of Social Services. Mayer and Timms' study *The Client Speaks* (1970) and Rees' later work *Social Work Face to Face* (1978) concentrate on the perceptions of white clients. There is a pressing need for further investigation – on a practical 'micro' level at Area Offices, and on a wider comparative level nationally.

Relevance

'The understanding reached is not self-evidently present in the problem itself. What is seen and done will depend upon the explanatory framework held. Shift the framework and its grid of understanding and the situation is perceived anew.' (Howe, 1987 p. 15).

Theories of social work, and hence practice have undergone many changes which to an extent parallel and reflect developments in the social sciences and changes in government policy, as well as the practical experience of social workers. Very recently, there have been the beginnings of a theory of social work rooted in black perspectives, some of which are drawn on in this chapter.

Much of the theory, however, which has underlain social work practice – from psychoanalytic and learning theory to gestalt therapy and transactional analysis, interactionism and Marxism is based on Western concepts and assumptions about behaviour. As Crescy Cannan notes:

'The principles and theories of social work need to be described as ideologies to be grounded in history and geography, and not taken as free floating legitimating ideas.' (Cannan, 1983 p.172).

The practical day-to-day decisions taken by social workers may have to take into account not only the client's interests but also broader issues such as policy consistency, the perceptions of the service held by clients in general, and the interests of the wider community. However, when working with clients from ethnic minorities, decision-making needs to be informed by the fact, that neither clients or 'the community' are homogeneous in terms of race, culture or language. This will impinge on the client's relationships with social workers, family, and the wider community. These relationships will be perceived, to varying degrees depending on the individual concerned, in terms of minority-majority relations. In other words, where the client is black and the social worker white, this perception will also form part of their interaction.

Without full knowledge of the context in which the client is operating, it is easy to make inappropriate decisions either because they are made in reference to what could be appropriate in a white, English context, or because the social worker's perceptions are influenced by stereotypes. Traditionally, social workers have been concerned to work with clients as unique individuals, while accepting that all human being have certain basic needs in common. Cultural differences between social workers and client present both with problems of interpretation of behaviour. The diagram 4.1 illustrates the relationship which may exist between three different levels of perception.

The experience of racism can affect clients at each of the levels in the diagram. But one particular difficulty for white social workers concerned to avoid unconscious racially biased assessments of clients is the problem of deciding how much weight to give to the cultural dimension in interpreting behaviour.

Shama Ahmed (BASW, 1987, p.6) gives the example of a one year old sick girl admitted to hospital with a fractured skull: 'At the case conference held by the health visitor, social workers and doctors, there was a tendency to assume that there is always a preference for male children in Asian cultures and so this small child must have been also unwanted, and therefore neglected. Later investigations showed that she was a much loved and long-awaited child of a somewhat slow mother who was unable to anticipate fully a growing child's activities and needs'.

Another example given by Ahmed is seen as typical of the way in which the difficulties of young Asians may be seen as a feature of their traditional cultures.

'A thirteen year old Asian girl was referred with a history of temper outbursts at home, refusing to speak to her father, use of abusive language, pilfering at home, the girl talked of her unhappiness at home having to do housework and washing clothes in cold water and

Table 4.1 Examples

Unique	Preferences Habits	Life-style Taste	Fears Pressures Adjustment Relationships Finance	Personality Projection Recognition- seeking Confidence	Values Motivation Contribution Achievement Growth	**Individual Level**
Different	Cooking Eating & Sleeping Customs	Houses Clothes	Living in groups Language Family Authority Attitudes to money	Names Status in family & community Forms of politeness	Religions Attitudes to work Patriotism	**Cultural Level**
Everyone needs:	(Life) Food Drink Sleep	Shelter Covering	Security Belonging Love	Identity Personal worth Self-respect	Purpose in Life Self-fulfilment	**Basic Human Level**

Acknowledgements to Sheila Cogill, Pathway Industrial Unit so on. This was quickly seen as a case of culture clash and it was said that the girl was showing identification with English girls and their way of life. Reactive depression was diagnosed but this was related to a culture clash, yet later investigation revealed many complications and a history of sexual advances by the father.' (p.6).

On the other hand, cultural information can be both relevant and useful. In one case at the Southall office, the interpreter was able to advise a social worker, correctly, to be much firmer with a client's son because he was the eldest and, as such, had certain responsibilities.

Crescy Cannan (1983, p.169) suggests, that the Western principles of self-determination and individualism are often inappropriate when working with clients from India. She suggests that these notions do not fit in well with the view of individuals as part of a corporate identity of family, village, caste. Often mutual obligations and duties will be stressed rather than individual rights. 'Thus the social worker's contribution to stresses within the family or joint family may lie in strengthening the bonds within the family who may be unduly repressive in their expectations, for instance of a young wife observing "purdah" or bearing an excessive number of children. Self-determination then is not irrelevant, but it is not akin to the Western view of personal fulfilment.'

Mental health social work provides numerous examples of the difficulties faced by social workers and psychiatrists in making appropriate decisions about the mental state of their clients/patients. The problem is often to decide whether behaviour should be interpreted at the individual or the cultural level. An example is the use of magical explanations, which may be common among people from rural backgrounds. The client may express a fear of someone using black magic or trying to poison him or her, and it will be for the social worker to decide whether this is a culturally normal way of expressing anxiety, or whether the client is suffering from paranoid delusions.

Language itself may influence the presentation of problems and, consequently, their assessment. It is not easy to find a precise way of expressing the English word 'depression', for instance, in Asian languages. The English reader will understand the difficulty if he or she tries to find a one-word equivalent in English. Words like 'sadness', 'misery', 'low spirits', 'a heavy heart' do not have the connotations of an identifiable medical state which are conveyed by 'depression'. The lengthy dictionary definition of the word – 'an emotional state of mind characterised by feelings of gloom and inadequacy, leading to withdrawal' – indicates how complex yet precise a meaning it carries. Whereas a white English client may tell his or her social worker 'I'm depressed', an Asian client with little or no English is likely to use colloquial equivalents of 'low spirits' or a 'heavy heart' which do not necessarily send the same signals when interpreted.

The role of the interpreter in such cases can be crucial, since the choice of words – particularly to describe feelings – can have a significant influence on the social worker's assessment decisions. Because language, behaviour and cultural context are so closely connected, it can, on occasions, be difficult for the white social worker to decide how far to rely on the interpreter for assistance. In interviews with social workers at the Southall Area Office, attitudes towards the interpreter's role in this respect fell somewhere between the following extremes:

A ←————————————————————→ B

| Total reliance on the inter-preter to explain attitudes and behaviour of the client | Interpreter's function per-ceived as simply translating words. Assumptions about the client's beliefs and customs usually not questioned |

Over reliance on the interpreter (that is, attitudes tending too far towards (A)), can result from the social worker lacking confidence in his or her judgement or, in some cases, from a reluctance to 'get close to' the client's culture. The other extreme (B), can result from a lack of trust on the part of the social worker for the interpreter, or, in some cases, a 'protectionist' attitude to the social worker role resulting in a reluctance to 'let the interpreter in' to the assessment process.

Clearly, the final responsibility for assessment rests with the social worker, and (A) is therefore to be avoided. However, the risk of wrong assessment inherent in (B) makes this approach probably more dangerous than (A). Generally, the majority of social workers inter-viewed aimed for a co-operative relationship with the interprepreter where both were able to evaluate each others' perceptions about clients in the light of what they knew about each other. A close working relationship based on a mutual awareness of the dangers of glib over-simplifications appeared to be the key to an effective partnership, coupled with a willingness to give the client every opportunity to express feelings, beliefs and attitudes direct.

Effectiveness

Apart from the improved communication which can derive from working through a trained interpreter, the social workers interviewed at the Southall office identified a number of other ways in which working through an interpreter can enhance the effectiveness of the service which an Area Office can offer to Asian clients.

It was easier for social workers to explain their roles and also the purpose and expected outcomes of the visit or interview.

Clients may come to social services unsure of what to expect and the interpreter can help here, as well as noticing when the client has misunderstood. In order for trust to develop, it is important for social workers to be able to communicate the reasons for their involvement, for any decisions they take, and the extent of their powers.

An important aim of social work is to help clients to help themselves. In order to be able to work together effectively on defining problems and arriving at solutions, both client and social worker have to be able to communicate effectively. The interpreter is a vital link here especially as the language used for this purpose is likely to be complex: negotiating, asserting oneself, describing difficult situations, challenging, and making suggestions.

In the area of mental health social work, it is suggested that approved social workers from a different ethnic group to the patient may need the help of members of the same group to understand disturbed behaviour. In this context it is clearly important that an adequate social history be obtained, and an interpreter will be essential where the client or the client's family speak little English. They may also have a suspicion of outsiders or authorities. Taking an interpreter along will not only ease the communications problems, but clients may well feel more comfortable about talking to the social worker.

A mental health referral may be delayed until a crisis has been reached, and the client may well be in a confused or distressed state. As already mentioned, the ability to speak in a second language is often affected by stress situations and a client whose English is normally good enough for everyday situations, may need the assistance of an interpreter when under stress. Good communication is an essential requirement for making correct assessments, diagnosing psychiatric illness and providing appropriate treatment. This can have important legal implications (as described in Chapter 3), particularly where the liberty of an individual is involved. Litlewood and Lipsedge point out 'Spanish speaking patients in New York have more symptoms when interviewed in English than when interviewed in Spanish, even when the psychiatrists use a special rating scale. This may be partly because what is quite a natural characteristic when speaking an unfamiliar language – slow speech with long pauses between words – is also a symptom of depression. However, these patients were rated as abnormal on all types of symptoms.' They further suggest that the social class and race of the doctor can affect the communication of problems, 'Patients are most likely to explore their feelings if the therapist is similar to them in ethnic group and class background'. (Littlewood and Lipsedge, 1982, p.118).

In the absence of a social worker from the same ethnic background as the client, the presence of an interpreter may help the client to open up and feel safe.

The last point has a relevance for counselling situations, where the growth of a relationship built on trust is so important. Good counselling involves effective listening and this in turn requires a good understanding of non-verbal communication. A trained interpreter can pick up these 'clues' and convey them appropriately to the social worker.

Interestingly, some of the social workers interviewed found that the slower pace of an interview through an interpreter was an advantage in some cases. They felt that they had more time to think and reflect during the interview and this often resulted in the interview being better structured.

Some social workers felt that two opinions can make for a more objective assessment and cut down on value judgements. Similarly the presence of interpreters at case conferences can make white social workers more aware of the danger of making prejudiced or racist assessments. This should not, of course, reduce the responsibility that white social workers have for challenging either their own or others' prejudice or racism.

There are a variety of para-professional roles which it can be useful for the interpreter to adopt. In addition to out-reach work in publicising the services offered, they can become involved in follow-up work. Ahmed (p.21) also suggests that they may have special focus duties such as developing group work with Asian women or Asian elderly people. The sharing of language and culture with clients can only be of benefit to the service.

Conclusions

We have explored the ways in which the provision of interpreting services can enhance good social work practice in three main areas: accessibility, relevance and effectivenes.

Interviews with Asian clients at the Southall Social Services Area Office indicated that the availability of interpreters made the office more accessible to clients whose first language was not English. This was reflected in the majority view that an interpreter employed by Social Services would be preferable to either a community or family interpreter.

It is recognised, however, that accessibility can only develop further if the demand for and use of interpreters is carefully monitored by Departments.

Interpreters can play an important role in helping social services to become more relevant to the black community. They have a role in bringing new perspectives to Departments and in clarifying cultural issues where conflicts of interest or understanding exist between social worker and client. However, the parameters of working relationship between social worker and interpreter need to be carefully defined.

In addition to the above we feel that, the provision of interpreting services can improve the effectiveness of social work practice in a variety of ways. Communication should improve overall and this in turn can help the development of more open and trusting relationships between social worker and client. Co-operation in defining problems and finding solutions is easier to achieve if both social worker and client can communicate in their own first language, through an interpreter. This is particularly important in mental health social work practice where good communication is vital for appropriate diagnosis and treatment.

Finally, interpreters can help develop the effectiveness of practice as a whole by, if agreed, taking on para-professional roles, thereby ensuring that links with the black community are strengthened and important information exchanges take place.

Chapter 5

Current Practice in
Local Authorities

Introduction

In March 1988, the Association of Directors of Social Services sent Pathway's questionnaire on interpreting provision to eighty-five Social Services departments serving multi-racial populations. Fifty-one questionnaires were returned – a response-rate of 60% – and although the survey was therefore not comprehensive, it does represent a significant sample of policy and practice.

Seventy-four (92%) of the departments who responded used the services of an interpreter in the course of their work although the degree of use varied, depending on:

1) The extent of the need and demand in the communities served.
2) The extent of interpreting provision made by the local authority.

There was clearly a dynamic in play between these two factors, and also between them and questions of resources and priorities. However, the purpose of the survey was to build up a 'snapshot' picture of current practice, rather than to conduct a detailed investigation into local conditions and decision-making. In fact the overall picture which emerged was one of growth and development in the awareness of the need for interpreters and a sense of responsibility for providing them. It is the practical aspects of this development which are described in this chapter.

We examine the different motivations for the employment of interpreters and the relationship between this and the employment of bilingual staff. We suggest a three-stage model of the way interpreters' roles may change as more bilingual staff enter the service.

We also examine the extent to which local authorities are monitoring the use made of their interpreting service, with particular reference to the monitoring requirements of Section 11 funding.

The type of interpreting provision made will naturally vary depending on the nature of local needs and spending priorities. The location of the interpreters, whether centrally, or in a particular department, or in a community organisation, will be an important determinant of the kind of service which the public receive. We evaluate the pros and cons of five different models of interpreting provision.

We also look at current practice in relation to sessional inter-preters – in particular where selection and training are concerned – and we examine the implications of drawing on the skills of bilingual staff to do interpreting on an ad hoc basis in addition to their other duties.

Employment of Interpreters

In 1988 twenty local authorities (39%) were already employing interpreters on a full-time or part-time basis. The number of posts listed in Table 5.1 below represents a considerable increase on the findings of ADSS' 1982 survey *Social Services and Ethnic Minorities*. At that time an analysis of the job titles of one hundred and ten specialist staff employed to work with ethnic minority clients – supplied by thirty-six Social Services Department revealed only one interpreter. (ADSS 1982 p.7. and fig. 4). A further six authorities had applications for Section 11 funding for interpreters under consideration by the Home Office at the time of the survey, and, in all, sixteen authorities in addition to those in the table were actively considering the issue and/or planning to make provision.

Section 11 was the main source of funding used, reflecting the increase in Social Services use of this resource in the eighties (only a quarter of the departments surveyed by the joint ADSS/CRE working group in 1978 had employed Section 11 staff. By the time of the 1982 ADSS survey, 53% of the authorities responding had specialist ethnic minority posts funded under Section 11.)

An interesting variant was provided by Greenwich Social Services, who were mounting a joint project with Greenwich Health Authority in response to the demands of Asian, Chinese and Vietnamese workers and organisations in the borough. Funding had been obtained from both Section 11 and Joint Finance. The interpreters were to be employed by Social Services and to be based in a Hospital Social Work team, with guidance from an Advisory Group including representatives of community organisations. The service was also to be represented on the Health Authority's established Working Party on Race and Health, and would report annually to the Joint Care Planning Team.

Two authorities were funding interpreting posts via MSC Community Programme. Since then, CP has been replaced by the Employment Training scheme, and MSC itself has been replaced by the Department of Employment's Training Agency.

The Policy Context – Reasons for Employing Interpreters

All the local authorities who participated had a formal Equal Opportunities Policy. Twenty-eight (55%) also had a race equality policy and

Table 5.1 Employment of Interpreters 1988

Authority	No. of Staff F/T	No. of Staff P/T	Location
Avon	–	2	Social Services
Berks (Slough)	–	1	Social Services
Birmingham	3	–	Social Services
Bolton	2	–	Central Unit
Bradford	–	4	Social Services
Brent*	2	–	Race Relations Unit
Coventry	5	–	Social Services
Ealing*	7	–	Social Services (2) Race Equality Unit (5)
Gloucestershire	–	6	County Sec. Dept.
Greenwich**	4	–	Hospital Social Work Team
Kensington & Chelsea	1	–	Central Service
Manchester	3	–	Social Services
Merton	1	–	Chief Executive's Department
Rochdale	3	–	Central Unit
Sandwell	6*	–	Social Services
Sheffield	7	2	Race Equality Unit (5) Education (4)
Southwark	4	–	Social Services
Strathclyde	2	2	Adjacent Strathclyde Comm. Relations Coun.
Surrey (Woking)	1	–	Social Services
Wolverhampton	–	7	Social Services (5) Environ. Health (2)
Totals	51	24	

* The Race Equality Unit in Ealing also had five translators and the Brent Unit had two, in addition to the posts listed.

** Greenwich also had a translation service in the Chief Executive's Department.

plan for the Social Services department. Thirteen of the latter already employed permanent interpreting staff and the remaining fifteen were either planning to employ interpreters or actively reviewing the issue. Although not all the twenty local authorities who employed interpreters had a departmental race equality policy and plan, a significant proportion did so, and the positive attention being given to the issue by the other fifteen authorities suggests that the process of drawing up such a policy and plan may well alert managers to unmet needs for interpreting provision.

We have noted previously (Chapter 2) that the existence of ethnic monitoring of staff and clients can provide a useful indication of the extent to which local authorities take their policies seriously. It is difficult to do much to implement a policy – still less to check if it is working – unless a system of ethnic record-keeping is in operation.

Twelve of the twenty authorities employing interpreters had already introduced ethnic monitoring of staff and 7 were also monitoring the ethnic origin of clients. It was difficult to gauge how far this had contributed to the decision to provide an interpreting service – funding submissions tended to quote census data and results of schools language surveys rather than the results of in-house monitoring. It seems more likely that an awareness of language need and of the need to monitor client characteristics developed in tandem as a result of reviews of departmental policy. A number of authorities had gone through a process of this kind.

It is important for any local authority employing interpreters to be clear about why this is being proposed, what it wants to achieve, and how this fits into the authority's wider equal opportunities strategy. The appointment of interpreters can be a functional adjunct to an overall policy of employing representative proportions of black staff (including bilingual staff). Or it can be an excuse for continuing to employ mostly white staff, in spite of the existence of a substantial black clientele. The decision to look at interpreting provision as an issue may itself have been provoked by the consequences of recruitment and training policies which had led to very few black staff being appointed. To appoint interpreters without also addressing this basic issue would look very much like 'papering over the cracks'.

Some of the Social Services departments who responded to the survey had linked the development of interpreting provision with an appraisal of the current and potential role of black bilingual staff in the department.

Apart from a review of basic recruitment and training practices in the context of equal opportunities legislation and practice, this may involve consideration of issues such as:

1) To what extent should ability to speak an ethnic minority language be a Genuine Occupational Qualification in the defining of social workers' jobs? (Race Relations Act, 1976 s.5.2.).
2) Does the department want to ensure that the proportion of ethnic minority social workers is at least the same as the proportion of ethnic minority residents in the area served? (this will have implications for training policies – Race Relations Act S.38).
3) What would be the implication of matching ethnic minority social workers with ethnic minority clients, given that it would not be acceptable to match white social workers with white clients?

In this context, it may also be useful for the department to establish a staged progression for the role of interpreters.

Stage 1: Where the majority of staff are white, there will be a clear need for comprehensive interpreting services.

During this period the department may want to recruit and train interpreters with a guarantee of eventual secondment to social work training (some authorities have a similar arrangement for Social Work Assistant Posts). This would be part of a general overhaul of recruitment and training policies which would also develop more direct routes to social work posts (and training) for Asian applicants.

Stage 2: As the proportion of ethnic minority to white social workers increases, roles should be re-defined and new responses generated to the contibution, needs and perceptions of the ethnic minority staff, and to development of new policies on service delivery. Interpreters will have an important contribution to make both as ethnic minority employees and colleagues, as well as acting as intermediaries between the office and the community.

Stage 3: Where the racial composition of the department and its local teams has become more balanced, the need for interpreters is likely to decrease. However, interpreters will continue to be needed in some areas for a number of reasons:

1) The proportion of white staff who continue to be employed.
2) The fact that ethnic minority staff are not usually equally competent in several different languages.
3) Situations where ethnic minority social worker and client meet a white monolingual third party (*eg.* a white judge or magistrate) and there are professional and ethical reasons for separating the social work and interpreting functions.

In summary, the recruitment and training of interpreters should be seen as part and parcel of an overall review of the relationship between staffing and service delivery. It is essential as an interim measure while longer term staffing policy changes are implemented, and interpreters can make an important contribution to the organisational development process this implies. In the longer term, interpreters will still be needed, but probably on a smaller scale, with some specialised functions.

Monitoring the Use of Interpreters

If the kind of development process outlined above is to take place, it will be important for the Social Services department to monitor the demand for interpreting services, and the extent to which this is met. Twelve of the local authorities who employed interpreters at the time of the survey kept figures of a sort, but these were not usually comprehensive in coverage or collated in a meaningful way. Several of the others employing interpreters said they planned to monitor the use of the service, but the overall picture which emerged was of monitoring taking place more by accident than by design. Of all the local authorities participating only twenty (39%) kept some kind of record of the

Table 5.2

Demand for Interpreting Services	No. of Local Authorities who monitored
Numbers of clients requesting an interpreter	9
Numbers of staff requesting an interpreter	14
Numbers of requests met	16

Interpreting sessions:
  by type of case
  by language used
  by type of service required
  (i.e. interpreting or translation)
	
	6
	15
	10

Total authorities carrying out any kind of monitoring	20

demand for or use of interpreting services, even though all used interpreters to varying degrees.

Most of the authorities who kept records (but by no means all) were able to account for the number of requests met and which language had been used. But requests from social workers were recorded more frequently than those from clients. This form of recording may obscure instances where social workers or receptionists are refusing or 'filtering out' requests for an interpreter, or where an interpreting service is overstretched and a certain amount of 'rationing' is going on.

It is important to keep a record of the types of cases which an interpreter is needed so that the department can establish the extent to which statutory functions are affected by communication difficulties, as well as collecting information about the nature of the work which may help in recruitment and training decisions, for both interpreters and social workers. The fact that less than a third of those who monitored paid any attention to this point suggests that many authorities have only a limited notion of the benefits of training interpreters in departmental procedures and in interpersonal aspects of service delivery, particularly where sensitive social work situations such as child abuse or mental health may be encountered. It is of particular concern that over 60% of participating authorities kept no records at all of their interpreting provision. Nine of these thirty-one were among those who had no provision other than sessional interpreters at the time of the survey, but stated that they were reviewing the situation. In the absence of any records of the demand, they were presumably going to make informed guesses on the basis of census and/or schools language survey data. It seemed a pity that the more accurate picture of needs which can be provided by careful monitoring of sessional interpreting had been foregone. (An example is given on page 114).

Conclusions

In general, local authorities' policies on keeping records of interpreting provision were often linked with their policies on ethnic monitoring. Both appeared to depend on the extent to which general equal opportunities policies had been implemented at departmental level. The survey results indicated that although a significant proportion of authorities had little more than a policy statement, the trend was towards monitoring and practical implementation.

Location of Interpreters

The decision of a public authority to locate its permanent interpreting provision in a particular department, or centrally, or in a community organisation is an important determinant of the kind of service which the public will receive.

In this section we examine five types of different approaches to the issue of location:

Type 1: a single, central co-ordinating post

This approach consists of the creation of a post of interpreting co-ordinator, often in the chief executive's department or central services, with the responsibility for linking requests for interpreting from service departments with sessional interpreters who are recruited onto a register.

The rationale is generally that a great variety of languages are spoken by minority groups in the area and that to employ one or two interpreters speaking between them a limited number of languages, would not provide as much coverage as the sessional approach. In the London Borough of Merton, for example, pilot translation and interpreting projects carried out with borough funding by the CRC and the CAB in 1984–85 identified a need for facilities in Hindi, Bengali, Tamil, Gujarati, Urdu, Panjabi, Vietnamese, Cantonese, Korean, Arabic, Greek, Spanish, Turkish, Polish, German, Russian and Thai, and it was pointed out that applications to primary schools in the borough indicated a range of fifty-four languages among children whose first language was not English. Clearly it would not be necessary or feasible to employ permanent full-time interpreters in all these languages, and a co-ordinated sessional approach would seem to be the best solution.

The limitation of this kind of provision is that there is a built-in delay between request and delivery. The interpreter is unlikely to be in the same building and the client who needs help may have to be referred elsewhere or make an appointment to see someone from the sessional register. It is certainly not geared up to deal with emergencies when the organisation may need to fall back on the services of bilingual staff – assuming that the relevant languages are available.

On the other hand, it is difficult to envisage any alternative where the spread of languages is so broad.

Type 2: Central interpreting function offering main languages, supplemented by sessional interpreters

Where there is a significant demand for particular languages spoken by a sufficiently large number of people, it becomes justifiable to employ full-time interpreters.

London Borough of Brent, for example, employed two interpreters centrally, offering between them the four main South Asian languages spoken in the borough – Gujarati, Panjabi, Hindi and Urdu – and their services in these languages were augmented as necessary by sessional interpreters. This ensured an experienced professional core of service provision while enabling the service to respond to more than two requests at the same time where need be. The register of sessional interpreters also covered the large number of other languages spoken by comparatively small numbers of people.

Part of the rationale for central provision may also be that departmentally-based interpreters are at risk of being monopolised by their service department and if the authority as a whole needs an interpreting service it should be based centrally so as to have maximum availability. It is also sometimes suggested that a central unit may be perceived by the community as more impartial than a departmentally based service.

The success of the model will depend very much on adequate resourcing and effective communication between the central unit and service departments. It does have the virtue of the co-ordination being carried out by practising interpreters, which was not necessarily the case with type one. They are likely to be better placed to select and train sessional interpreters.

Type 3: Central interpreting function plus sessional interpreters based in a community organisation

In July 1980 Strathclyde Interpreting Service opened in Glasgow with Urban Aid funding, managed by Strathclyde Community Relations Council. In 1988, on the expiry of Urban Aid, Strathclyde Regional Council took over funding of the service on the grounds that it had become 'an indispensible resource' (SRC, 1987 p.10). The staff – two full-time and two part-time interpreters – became employees of the Regional Council as from 1.4.88 and management responsibility rested with the Social Work department. However, the service was still based at the CRC office and had an advisory committee, chaired by the CRC, consisting of representatives of both statutory and voluntary user groups.

Accessibility is clearly the main advantage of a community-based service, and there is a sharp contrast with departmentally-based interpreting services which may only provide assistance to clients of the department or of the local authority. However, resources are likely to be particularly stretched as a result of an 'open door' policy. Unless such a service is well staffed, waiting-time may increase to unacceptable levels. Emergencies arising in the evenings and at weekends may put staff under additional pressure.

'A further difficulty arises if the interpreting officers are undertaking duties outside the office. The budget has not been sufficient to employ casual interpreters to staff the office at such times and work is so unpredictable that it would be impractical to publicise set hours at which officers fluent in the main languages are on duty.

Claims on the service from the court present special problems because they are often made at the last minute, and a refusal to provide a service would cause unnecessary inconvenience for the person(s) involved. On some occasions interpreting officers have found themselves detained at court hearings on serious matters for days at a time, throwing plans for other work out of schedule completely. So far as possible casual interpreters are used for court and childrens' hearing work, but it is not always easy to maintain the necessary quality control' (SRC, 1987 p.3.)

These kinds of problem are frequently encountered by interpreting services with a core of paid staff supplemented by sessional interpreters, and they are likely to increase in direct proportion to the service's accessibility to the public. A clear policy on staffing organisation and the provision of adequate resources is essential if staff are to be retained and the service is to remain effective in such circumstances.

Strathclyde Interpreting Service deal with a wide variety of cases, examples of which include:

1) A family dispute which resulted in police intervention and social work involvement. SIS help with interpreting and mediation resulted in a peaceful outcome.
2) Translation of an information booklet for Yorkhill Hospital.
3) Help with organisation of Asian Womens' Health Fair.
4) Assistance in translating letters and claim forms for Social Work Department single payments campaign.
5) Translation of crime prevention leaflet.
6) Interpreting at parent/teacher meetings in schools.
7) Help to a middle-aged woman found wandering in the street, who had a record of mental illness. Liaison with the Homeless Persons Unit and Social Work department.
8) Involvement with children received into residential care, including participation in joint sessions with social workers and parents.
9) Meeting with DHSS publicity officer for Scotland to explore avenues of creating greater awareness of entitlements.

10) Assistance to a woman in fighting a case for access to, and custody of, her child over a three year period, involving sessions with court, social workers, housing department, DHSS, lawyer, landlord, language teacher, health clinic and GP.

11) An emergency referral from a mother and her three children who had been subject to ill-treatment and physical assault. The case involved arranging for medical treatment for post-natal depression, interviews with husband and liaison with Social Work department.

12) Help to the child guidance service over a 6 year old child with behavioural problems, and subsequent assistance to the family over other underlying marital and health problems.

13) Interpreting sessions with a family of ten children, three of whom had been before the Children's Panel, to attempt to overcome problems of clashing cultures.

Direct funding of a community-based interpreting service by a Social Services department who also perform a management function, as in the case of SIS from 1988, may, however, make it difficult for impartiality to be maintained in cases such as the dispute over access cited above. Ultimately, the interpreter must be acceptable to both parties – or each must provide his or her own.

SIS charged some of the statutory organisations for whom work was undertaken. No charge was made to Strathclyde Regional Council, as the sponsoring authority, or to individuals. Payments made for the services of sessional interpreters were generally passed direct to the interpreters.

If one of the prime objectives of a community-based interpreting service is to increase accessibility to individuals, then it will clearly not be possible for fees charged to cover more than a small proportion of the costs of the service.

The Strathclyde service was one of the earliest interpreting services to be established in the UK, and its more recent combination of community location with Council funding and management make it of particular interest as a model especially as regards local authority/ CRC co-operation.

Type 4: Interpreters in Social Services department offering main languages supplemented by sessional interpreters and/or bilingual staff as necessary.

The main advantages of this model are

1) The availability of the interpreter at the point of service delivery (for the majority of users).

2) The expertise developed by the interpreter about the dynamics of social work situations.

London Borough of Ealing had employed two interpreters based at its Southall Social Services office, since 1985. A duty rota operated so that someone was available to interpret five days a week. Both interpreters spoke Panjabi, the language of the vast majority of the Southall office's clients, and between them, Urdu and Hindi. Other languages were covered by sessional interpreters and contacts with other agencies such as the Greater London Translation Service.

It was felt that employing the interpreters full-time meant that they were able to become familiar with departmental procedures, jargon, practices and situations. Equally important, they were able to develop trust, mutual understanding and effective working relationships with individual social workers. This made the interpreting process more efficient, but also meant that other aspects of the interpreter's role such as explanation of cultural factors, or contributing to assessment became more effective. Some social workers found it especially useful to be able to work with the same interpreter on a particular case over a long period. Although this sometimes occurred with sessional interpreters, the relationship was more limited, being largely restricted to contact over one case. Social workers felt that work with the departmental interpreter on certain cases was informed by other joint work previously undertaken.

There is some evidence that interpreters based at one Area Office may be underused by staff at other offices. Although Southall's two interpreters were, in principle, available to the whole department, an analysis of the 1987 workload showed that 95% of clients for whom interpreting was undertaken lived in the Southall office's catchment area. Half of the remainder had lived in the area before moving and were still seeing Southall social workers. The availability of the interpreting service was well-known and in fact one of the interpreters contributed an hour to the department's induction programme for new staff. Lack of knowledge about the service was therefore an unlikely explanation. Other possible explanations included:

1) A tendency for social workers in other areas to try to 'get by' without an interpreter because of the extra time involved in contacting the latter and arranging an appointment.
2) The use of bilingual staff as an immediate 'on-site' resource, rather than call an interpreter and defer action.
3) Less demand in other offices.

Although it was true that there was lower take-up of services by Asian clients at the other Social Services offices, this was not sufficient in itself to explain the difference in use of the interpreting facility. The interpreters' own experience pointed to the two other explanations, and this would suggest that the choice of location for interpreters is important not only in terms of efficient service delivery, but also in terms of social workers' awareness of the potential of working with interpreters, and the limitations of communicating without one where there is a language difficulty.

Where a Social Services department employs interpreters in the absence of any other provision by the local authority this may stimulate demand from other departments such as housing or education. In this situation, managers may find that they are forced into a 'protective' stance, which may make what was in fact an innovatory move begin to look like parochialism. If this arises, it will be important for the departmental manager to encourage a corporate assessment of needs and provision. Problems arising from the availability of a service are, however, infinitely preferable to those which arise when no service is provided, and this model has much to recommend it, in particular from the potential it offers for integrating the interpreting function into the overall service delivery strategy of the department at both management and casework levels.

Type 5: Central interpreting/translation function plus departmentally-based interpreters

After the establishment of Ealing's two interpreting posts in the Social Services department, and a change of administration, the borough established a central Language Section consisting of ten interpreters and translators in the Race Equality Unit. The existence of this central resource allowed the Social Service interpreters to concentrate on work within their department without the pressure to assist housing, education or any other part of the local authority's operation which might otherwise have developed.

Sheffield also had type 5 provision, although the departmentally-based interpreters were in Education rather than Social Services. The Central Race Equality Unit, offered Bengali, Urdu, Arabic and Chinese interpreting and other languages through a register of sessional interpreters. The Multi-cultural Education Service also had three full-time and two part-time posts, offering the same languages. Whereas the Race Equality Unit interpreters' remit was to offer an authority-wide service, the latter concentrated on Education-related situations.

In Sandwell, which was about to appoint six full-time interpreters in the Social Service department there was a parallel development in the Chief Executive's department to create a centrally-based Translation and Interpreting Service which would work not only for the authority as a whole, but also be available to other statutory bodies such as Police, Probation, Health Authority, Courts, Fire and Civil Defence, and also to ethnic minority organisations and voluntary organisations in general. This move was seen as complementary to departmental provision.

There are initial indications that this model is likely to become the most appropriate for local authorities with a high proportion of residents who speak languages other than English. The departmentally- based interpreters are able to develop service-related expertise and integrate their skills with those of other professionals to provide an efficient service to clients of that particular service. They can be located at the point of service delivery, so as to maximise their availibility and to signal to users that communication in a language other than English is welcomed. The centrally based interpreters can adopt a more strategic role, addressing authority-wide issues of communication and providing, where appropriate, a service to non-Council bodies such as those indicated by Sandwell.

The central unit in Sandwell seemed likely to focus more on translation of documents, at least initially, and there are strong arguments for this function being centralised, provided communication with service departments is good:

1) A group of translators, centrally located, can provide each other with back-up and support, and pool expertise.
2) It will enable the development of a consistent style, reflecting corporate image and objectives, in minority languages as well as in English.
3) Expensive technological resources, such as Gurmukhi or Hindi typesetting equipment, can be centrally located to achieve maximum accessibility and usage.
4) Translators can be involved in the drafting stage of documents, leaflets, posters etc. so that their expertise in written communication can benefit the authority's overall public relations policy and practice.

Translation involves skills which are rather different from those needed to interpret – sufficiently different to justify the assertion that a good translator does not necessarily make a good interpreter and vice versa (see p. 119 for fuller discussion). This in itself suggests that a central unit for translation is likely to be more effective than what is still frequently the pattern – that is, departmentally based interpreters being asked to undertake the occasional piece of translation. Not only will they not necessarily have the skills, but they may also be pressed for time. The result of such an arrangement may be that translation requirements are marginalised by the immediacy of clients' needs for interpreting.

For less frequently needed languages, it will be more efficient for a register of sessional translators and interpreters to be maintained centrally, than for each department to try to do this individually. The central unit can then ensure consistent standards by adopting standardised selection criteria and methods for individuals and organisations offering their services on a sessional basis. It will often also be appropriate for the central unit to co-ordinate, and in some instances deliver training for sessional interpreters, in conjunction with full-time interpreters based in departments. In addition, the central unit will be able to offer expertise to departments concerning the recruitment and deployment of the latter. A well-developed central unit should be monitoring the demand for and usage of interpreters authority wide, and making recommendations for changes or further development as required.

Who should provide Interpreting Services – views of Local Authorities

Respondents to the Pathway survey were asked who they thought was the most appropriate provider of the interpreting services. The answers are set out in Table 5.3 below:

Table 5.3

Most appropriate provider	Numbers	%
Local authority only	23	45
Local authority and other statutory or voluntary bodies	13	25
Local authority and CRC	3	6
Other community organisation	3	6
No answer/undecided	9	18
Totals	51	100

Local Authority only: reasons given

1) It is the authority's legal responsibility to provide interpreting facilities.
2) Interpreters can be available when required. A more efficient service.
3) Interpreters can develop departmental expertise.
4) Confidentiality of service can be maintained.
5) Ensures accountability and monitoring.
6) Better selection and training.
7) Gives professional recognition and career and structure to interpreters.
8) Some local authorities do not have a CRC.
9) CRC's often do not have the resources.

Mixed provision and community-based service: reasons given

1. Accessibility: service not restricted to users of the particular department where the interpreter is located.
2. Credibility: clients have more confidence in a community-based service, and interpreters more likely to offer sessional services.
3. Conflicts of interest – for instance in child protection or mental health situations – may make community provision more appropriate.
4. Independent body with its own management committee provides

better support for interpreters and is accountable for standards and quality.

The views of Community Relations Councils are given in Chapter 7.

Conclusions

Each of the five approaches described has some merits. Any organisation which may need an interpreter in a crisis situation, however, would be well advised to give serious consideration to employing interpreters at the point of service delivery, as in Type 4. It is clearly not effective to have to ask a client who is depressed and considering suicide to 'come back tomorrow when we've found an interpreter'. Unless an interpreter is available when this client comes to the office, the possibility of suicide may not even be identified until it is too late. Duty social workers should, in principle, be able to call upon a duty interpreter. In practice, of course, this will only be feasible where a language is spoken by a large number of clients. Languages which do not occur with any significant degree of frequency will need to be catered for by sessional interpreters or by bilingual staff. Choices about how far to rely on the latter as opposed to employing full-timers will be fundamental in the process of setting up any interpreting service.

Use of Sessional Interpreters

Thirty-nine authorities (76%) in the Pathway survey used the services of sessional interpreters, but there was some variation in the way these were used, as the tables below illustrate.

Table 5.4 Type of Use

Type of use	Number	% of total using sessional interpreters
To supplement full-time or part-time provision	10	26
In combination with bilingual staff who 'help out' with interpreting	21	54
Sessional interpreters only	8	20
Totals	39	100

Local authorities obtained their sessional interpreters from a variety of sources.

Table 5.5 Sources of Sessional Interpreters

Source	Number of Authorities
Register of individuals	17
Community interpreting service*	7
Community Relations Council	6
Voluntary and religious organisations	5
Police register	3
Embassy	1
Local Authority English Language Scheme	1
Totals	40

Community interpreting service indicates an organisation or service set up specifically for this purpose. In some cases this meant an MSC Community Programme, in others, a community organisation with local authority funding. Avon County Council, for instance, used Avon Community Interpreting Service, an Urban Aid funded project. Lothian Regional Council funded an independent interpreting and translation service jointly with Lothian Health Board and Edinburgh District Council.

Selection of Sessional Interpreters

The selection of sessional interpreters is extremely important. Misinterpretation can have serious consequences, as illustrated by the Birmingham City Council case which received front page publicity in 1987. (See Chapter 3.) Practice in local authorities is evolving slowly in the right direction, but in too many cases selection consists only of an interview carried out in English and another language. A conversation carried out in an Asian language is not a test of interpreting ability – only of fluency in the language concerned. Public authorities which 'take on trust' the abilities of sessional interpreters who put themselves forward for the register are taking a risk with the effectiveness of the service they provide. Surprisingly, twenty-three of the fifty-one Social Services departments surveyed by Pathway in 1988 still came into this category. (For a broader discussion of selection methods, see Chapter 3.)

A similarly rudimentary approach was found in many authorities as far as training for sessional interpreters was concerned. 70% of the authorities using sessional interpreters did not provide any training at all. In some cases it was not appreciated that training was necessary. It was taken for granted that fluency in both languages could be equated with interpreting ability. In other cases respondents did not appear to understand what training for interpreters might consist of, and several complained that there was no-one in their area who would be able to provide such training.

On the positive side, some local authorities were giving some attention to the problem, either by asking full-time interpreters to organise training for sessionals, or by setting up a course in conjunction with a local college. These two avenues are likely to be followed by an increasing number of organisations concerned to ensure that the service they deliver is of consistent quality. (For a fuller discussion of the training issues, see Chapter 8.)

Bilingual Staff who 'help out' with interpreting

We have argued earlier that the employment of interpreters should never be seen as a substitute for the employment of bilingual staff in proportions which reflect the local ethnic minority population. It is equally important, however, that bilingual staff should not be seen as a substitute for the employment of interpreters in certain circumstances.

Some authorities already employing interpreters also use the services of bilingual staff to interpret on occasions – when interpreters are not immediately available, or where a language is required which the interpreters do not have. The availability of these bilingual staff at the point of service delivery makes this an efficient means of supplementing the interpreting service. There would seem little point in calling in a sessional interpreter from outside if there is a bilingual employee in the office who can do the job. Provided it is an agreed part of their job description, and recognition, renumeration where appropriate, and training are given to such staff, then this would seem a sensible use of resources.

Twenty-five authorities in the Pathway survey – over 80% of those authorities who had no permanent interpreting posts at the time of the survey – said that bilingual staff helped out with interpreting. Twenty-one of these also used sessional interpreters.

There were a very few instances where these staff had interpreting duties included in their job descriptions. A few authorities wrote this into the job description of Social Work Assistants who had a specific brief to assist clients with language difficulties. Where they occurred these were usually Section 11 funded posts.

Otherwise, bilingual staff tended to help out, as one local authority put in, 'on a goodwill basis'. Only three authorities made any payment for the language service being provided, and, as another authority pointed out, these skills rarely seem to be counted as such in local authority job evaluation processes. London Borough of Ealing was the only instance where a systematic borough-wide scheme was being introduced. Employees on non-professional grades whose job description did not already include the use of language skills, but who were fluent in a language other than English and used this skill to a significant extent in the course of their work, were to receive a Language Supplement equal to 10% of salary. The possibility of providing training for staff receiving the supplement was being explored.

There are a number of dangers in relying on the 'goodwill' of bi-lingual staff:

1) Although fluent in both languages, they are unlikely to have been trained to interpret.

2) The skills involved are often taken for granted by mono-lingual staff. Bi-lingual staff may withdraw their goodwill if demands on their services become excessive.

3) The nature and extent to which their services are used is rarely monitored, and they may in fact be 'covering up' the real need for an interpreter to be employed.

One local authority stated that they had no plans to examine the need for interpreters or provide interpreting services because they 'would prefer to employ professionally trained social workers with languages rather than extending the use of interpreters *per se*'. (The Social Services department concerned used sessional interpreters from a variety of sources). This illustrates a frequently encountered misconception – that employing bilingual social workers is a substitute for employing interpreters.

At its worst, this practice can result in an ethnically-based division of labour in the office which is fundamentally unequal. Black and white social workers are placed on the same grades and the same pay scales. But the black bilingual social workers are expected to act as interpreters for the whites when the latter run into difficulties because they cannot communicate with certain clients. In other words, the black social worker's job includes a servicing or support role to the white social worker which the latter, with the best will in the world, cannot reciprocate. This can cause tensions on both sides.

In principle, the difficulty could be avoided by allocating clients with language difficulties to bilingual staff. This would, however, be just as inequitable since the latter would then have a narrower choice of clients than their white counterparts. It would also not necessarily be the best solution for clients for language to become the overiding criterion for allocation of cases.

It is very important for local authorities to employ bilingual social work staff. But they should be employed primarily for their professional skills as social workers and should use their language skills with their own clients as appropriate. As we have said earlier, the demand for interpreting should diminish as an office employs more bilingual staff. But in the meantime, it will be important for the latter – and their managers – to ensure that they are not 'disguising' the need for an interpreting post.

Bilingual Staff: Conclusions

Local authorities who use the services of bilingual staff to interpret on a goodwill basis should monitor the extent of this practice as part of a review of the need for proper interpreting provision. Where it is agreed that such arrangements should continue, they should be written into job evaluation schemes (where this is not already the case). Alternatively, a 'language supplement' scheme like Ealing's may be considered.

Chapter 6

Managing the Interpreting Function

In this chapter, we focus on the following practical aspects of managing the interpreting function:

Selection

Given the responsibilities carried by interpreters working in public services, recruitment methods are often still surprisingly haphazard – particularly when it comes to making a considered assessment of the applicant's interpreting skills. Many interpreters are still appointed on the basis of being able to converse fluently in English and another language during an interview.

The ability to hold a conversation is not the same as the ability to interpret, which needs a whole range of skills not required, or only partially required, in normal conversation.

An interview can of course be a valid means of assessing certain aspects of a candidate's application: for instance, reasons for applying, perceptions of what the job entails, career aspiratons, knowledge and experience of local authority procedures, views on ethical issues such as confidentiality. It is not, however, a valid means of testing aptitude or ability to interpret. Such a test requires controlled conditions where a number of different factors can be assessed. Interpreting accuracy needs to be tested over a minimum ten minute period, where the interaction can be recorded and played back for detailed checking later. In order to provide a more systematic basis for the assessment of interpreting skills – or at least, of interpreting aptitude, the authors devised and piloted a test for use by London Borough of Ealing Social Services department in appointing its interpreters. The procedures and marking system were piloted with groups of trainee interpreters through mid-course assessment tests and final examinations for Pathway's Diploma in Community Interpreting, as well as in the job selection context. The test is designed to be used in conjunction with a standard selection interview, but separately administered. It sets out to test oral interpreting ability in the following respects: accuracy; clarity; fluency; speed and process skills.

The level required is determined by the employing agency in relation to the job description and person specification. It will be for the latter to decide whether successful candidates should be of equivalent standard to a pass grade for the Diploma, or whether a lower standard is acceptable on the basis that in-service training will be provided.

Design of the Test

1) Candidates are asked to interpret (usually for ten minutes) between two 'users'.
   User A speaks English. User B speaks the appropriate community language. Both users must be able to role-play convincingly.
2) A new dialogue is written for each post to avoid any possibility of candidates having advance knowledge of the test. Each dialogue is designed to the following criteria:

    (i) The situation used must be relevant to the post advertised.
    (ii) Both English and the community language must be present in equal proportions and with equal levels of difficulty.
    (iii) The phraseology used must be typical of that likely to be encountered by the candidate in the post in question.

3) The content of the dialogue is identical for all candidates for a given post. Where slight digressions are unavoidable because of interpreting mistakes this is accounted for in the marking.

Administration of the Test

1) Candidates are briefed about the form of the test, the situation to be used and the skills being tested. *It is essential that all candidates understand this before taking the test.*
2) Candidates take the test one at a time in a separate room. There must be no contact between candidates who have taken it and those still waiting.
3) The test is recorded on audio-cassette and marked separately for accuracy, clarity, fluency and speed.
4) Marks are awarded immediately after each test for process skills. These are:

    (i) The ability to form an effective working relationship with both users, equally.
    (ii) Appropriate use of direct and indirect interpreting.
    (iii) Ability to check and clarify meaning appropriately.
    (iv) Ability to control the speed and quantity of information to be interpreted.
    (v) Ability to keep both users in touch with the proceedings throughout.
    (vi) Ability to switch appropriately from one language to another.

The test does not set out to assess more advanced features of interpreting ability, such as pre-interview briefing skills, the ability to deal with unpredictables (eg. an aggressive or tearful user) or the ability to intervene appropriately where the users appear to be misunderstanding one another. It would be neither feasible nor fair to candidates to introduce elements such as these in a job selection context.

Marks for these skills are awarded by User A, User B and one observer.

It is for the employer to decide how much weight to give to the test in the selection process. This will again depend on the job description and employee specification.

Testing Translation Skills

As already mentioned, the skills required for written translation are very different from those required for oral interpreting (see also Chapter 8). Essentially, a test of translation abilities should look for the following:

1 An ability to respond sensitively to the purpose of the original and to convey this faithfully in translation.
2) Sensitivity to style in the particular context, and an ability to produce an acceptable equivalent in translation.
3) An ability to write fluently, using plain language as far as the content of the original permits. Readability should be paramount, taking into account the likely level of the reader and the purpose of the document in question.
4) An ability to use reference books appropriately.

An example of an English-Panjabi translation test is given below.

English-Panjabi Translation Test

As an interpreter in the Social Services department, you will be required to translate leaflets for the public into clear, simple language, which anyone can understand.

The passage below is an extract from a leaflet:

INSTRUCTIONS

1) *Please translate the passage below into clear, simple Panjabi which anyone could understand.*
2) *Use the dictionary if you need to, but do not feel you must use it.*
3) *Please translate the whole passage and hand your work in when you are satisfied it will convey the meaning.*
4) *You can hand your work in at any time until*   .   _____

Social Workers have a duty by law, to make plans for all children in care whether their parents have agreed to them being in care or whether a court order has been made. Social Workers make plans for children all the time, but there are especially important meetings, called Reviews held at least every 6 months. You will usually be invited to the Review, or part of it, and it is particularly important that you attend. If you do not, the Social Worker will not know what your feelings are or what you think is right for your child. Most major decisions about your child's future will be made at Reviews and these could include when or whether she/he will return home, or whether any changes in the arrangements for you to see your child need to be made.

Sometimes, Social Workers will have to make decisions about children in care which they see as being in the child's best interests but which will be very upsetting to parents and with which parents may never agree. Such decisions may include stopping parents seeing their children either completely, or as often as they would like.

A Code of Practice for Social Workers Working through Interpreters

The employment of interpreters adds a third person to the typically one to one casework relationship (or one to group in family situations). Issues are likely to arise such as confidentiality, the extent to which the interpreter should contribute to assessment, what to do, where the department is in conflict with a client with limited English, and the client's right to ask for an interpreter or to do without one.

The Code of Practice which follows was evolved during four courses run by the authors for staff from London Borough of Ealing Social Services department. Participants on each course were invited to comment on the draft so far and to suggest improvements. The department's interpreters were involved throughout. The final draft was then considered by the department's senior management team, who adopted it as departmental policy in June 1988.

Although the Code is specific to the social work context, it is relevant to most interpreting contexts, and can be easily adapted to fit almost any other public sector situation. We have not attempted what would have been an impossible task – to devise a universally applicable Code – since, in our experience it is more useful for agencies to have their own service-specific Codes which can take account of the practicalities of the operating context.

However, it can be a great help to look at Codes which already exist as an aid to formulating one's own, and the Ealing Code is therefore given in full below. It is split into two parts – the first is for social workers working through an interpreter, and the second is for interpreters working for the department. The two parts are complementary.

Why a Code of Practice?

To Protect Social Work Clients

Social Services clients are more in need of protection than most consumers for a number of reasons:

1) In most cases the department is a 'monopoly supplier' and the client's choice of agency is strictly limited.
2) In some cases clients may be receiving attention from the department against their wishes.
3) The department has legal and quasi-legal functions and important decisions about peoples' lives are often made within the department and outside the framework of the courts.
4) As a result of disadvantage or handicap, clients may be in a poor position to fight for their rights.
   (drawn from NISW, 1982, Chapter 12).

All these factors become more acute if a client is unable to communicate directly with social work staff because of language difficulties. The decision to involve an interpreter, and the way the social worker uses the interpreter's services, can have a crucial effect on clients' understanding and exercise of their rights and responsibilities as citizens.

To Ensure Statutory Duties are Carried out Effectively

Many of the statutory provisions under which the department operates require staff to communicate with clients and other members of the public. If communication is not effective because of language difficulties, and an interpreter is not used, or the social worker fails to use the interpreter's services effectively, statutory requirements may not be met.

In addition, Section 71 of the Race Relations Act places a duty on local authorities to ensure that their functions are carried out with due regard to the need to (a) eliminate unlawful discrimination; and (b) promote equality of opportunity and good relations between persons of different racial groups.

Section 20 of the Act makes it unlawful for anyone who is concerned with the provision of goods, facilities or services to discriminate by (a) refusing or deliberately omitting to provide them; or (b) as regards their quality or the manner or the terms on which she or he provides them.

It is therefore essential that the department's staff know how and in what circumstances interpreters should be involved. Failure to recognise and act on the need for an interpreter, or ineffective use of an interpreter's services, could constitute discrimination in terms of the Race Relations Act.

To Protect Social Services Staff

The statutory context outlined above implies that the department has a duty to make clear to staff precisely what is expected of them, and to provide training as appropriate.

The British Association of Social Workers has a Code of Ethics to which members are committed. Its basic principles include 'the recognition of the value and dignity of every human being, irrespective of origin, status' sex, sexual orientation, age, belief or contribution to society' and a commitment not to 'act selectively towards clients out of prejudice.'

BASW's Code also commits members to:

1) Help clients increase the range of choices open to them and their power to make decisions.
2) Help clients to obtain all those services and rights to which they are entitled, both from the agency and from any other appropriate source.
3) Respect clients as individuals and to seek to ensure that their dignity, individuality, rights and responsibility are safeguarded.

The Code of Practice enables departments to inform social workers how these and other professional principles can be applied to and be affected by the use of interpreting services. Particular attention is paid to the issue of confidentiality.

To Protect Interpreters

Interpreters who are permanent employees of a Social Services Department and are working with other staff on a day-to-day basis need to know what they can expect of the latter and what is expected of them. This will help co-operation and the provision of a high standard of service to the public.

Interpreters who are not Council employees but are used on a sessional basis by the department may be unused to working in the kind of situations which arise in Social Services, and it will then be essential for the social worker involved to be able to give a clear lead as to how the interpreting should be carried out.

Code of Practice for Social Workers[*]

Basic Responsibility

The responsibility for ensuring effective communication between the Social Service department and any client rests with the social worker concerned.

The Decision to use an Interpreter

In deciding whether an interpreter is needed, the following criteria should be considered (subject to situations covered under *Emergencies* below).

1) *The client's wishes*

If clients feel they would be able to communicate more effectively through an interpreter, the social worker should arrange for this. If clients feel they do not need an interpreter, this should be respected.

However, where the client does not feel an interpreter is needed, but the social worker is not confident that effective communication will take place, it is for the social worker to decide whether to involve an interpreter or not, taking into account the other criteria such as statutory duties and equality of service.

2) *The social worker's statutory duties*

If the social worker has a duty to obtain or convey certain information and there is any doubt about the client's ability to communicate effectively in the social worker's language, an interpreter should be used.

3) *Equality of service delivery*

If there is any question of a client receiving a lesser service, in terms of quality or effectiveness, than that which would have been offered had the client's first language been the same as the social worker's, an interpreter should be provided.

Emergencies

In an emergency situation, where an interpreter is not available, and a delay might have serious consequences, it may be necessary for the social worker to act immediately, even though communication with the client is inadequate. In these circumstances, the social worker should arrange to see the client with an interpreter as soon as possible after action has been taken.

---

[*] *A note on terminology.*

(i) *In the draft Code, the term 'client' is used to mean anyone with whom the member of staff has a professional or statutory obligation to communicate.*

(ii) *The term 'social worker' is used as a general term to mean anyone employed by the Social Services department with a responsibility for direct communication with clients.*

Choice of Interpreter

The social worker should ensure that interpreting can take place in the client's first language

The only exception to this would be in an emergency situation (see above) where communication in a second language which client and interpreter have in common would be acceptable.

The interpreter must be acceptable to both social worker and client

The social worker should check that the interpreter is acceptable to the client at the earliest possible stage, so as to avoid delays and embarrassment. This applies whether the interpreter is employed by the department or not. (For examples of difficulties clients may have with particular interpreters, see *Commentary* p. 94)

The social worker should avoid using family members or friends of the client as interpreters. Apart from the fact that they are unlikely to have been trained to interpret, their involvement may undermine objectively and confidentiality.

If the client wishes a family member or friend to interpret, the social worker may agree to this in certain circumstances:

1) In a first interview, where the subject-matter is straightforward, brief and uncontroversial.
2) Where the client's confidence would be undermined by a refusal to accept his or her relative or friend as interpreter. In this case, however, the social worker may arrange for an independent interpreter also to be present.

In no circumstances should a relative or friend be accepted as interpreter where there might be a conflict of interest between interpreter and client.

Where the department is in conflict with the client and the latter doubts the impartiality of an interpreter provided by the department, the social worker should inform the client that he or she is free to obtain an independent interpreter. In these circumstances the social worker should provide the client with a list of agencies providing interpreting services, but it will be for the client to make contact with them.

If the client obtains his or her own interpreter in these circumstances, the social worker should be accompanied by a departmental interpreter, who will interpret for the social worker and check the accuracy of the client's interpreter.

Access to Interpreting Services

All reception areas used by the public should carry a notice in the relevant languages advertising the availability of an interpreting service.

Managers should ensure that social workers know the procedures for obtaining an interpreter. A list of voluntary organisations providing interpreting services should be readily accessible for situations where an in-house interpreter is not available.

Confidentiality

Interpreters working as permanent employees of the Social Services Department are bound by the same rules of confidentiality as other staff.

Interpreters who offer their services on a sessional basis should be reminded of the confidential nature of the work and be required to sign a written undertaking that they will:

1) Not divulge anything to any person not present during the interpreting process without the express permission of the social worker concerned.
2) Inform the social worker before the interpreting process begins if the client is personally known to them.

A copy of the form to be signed by sessional interpreters is attached (see *Commentary*). It should be signed before the interpreting process begins except in emergencies, in which case the social worker should arrange for signature as soon as possible afterwards.

Pre-Interview Briefing

It is essential for social worker and interpreter to agree the basis on which they will work together before the interpreting process starts. In particular, the social worker should make clear:

1) The identity of the people involved and their relationships with each other and with the social worker.
2) The purpose of the conversation to be interpreted. This may include relevant background information about the case.
3) The social worker's own objectives and desired outcomes, where appropriate.
4) How long the interpreting process is likely to last.
5) Any difficult language or concepts which are likely to arise.
6) Any difficult behaviour which may be encountered (*e.g.* anger, tearfulness, withdrawal) and how the interpreter should respond.

It is for the social worker to decide how much detail to include under points 2 and 3. In general, the better an interpreter is briefed, the more effectively she or he will interpret. Before withholding information the social worker should therefore be sure that (a) it will not help the interpreter during the conversation to be interpreted, or (b) there is a strong professional justification for not disclosing it.

Before the interpreting process begins, the social worker should also agree with the interpreter:

1) The style of interpreting which will be used (see *Commentary* p. 96).
2) How the initial introductions are to be carried out.

During the Interpreting Process

Full exchange of information
The interpreter's role is to convey the meaning of everything which is said.

This does not mean literal, word-for-word translation, but it does mean passing on the sense of what is said on both sides without omission.

This means that the social worker should:

1) Avoid saying anything to the interpreter which he or she does not want to be passed on to the client.
2) Make clear when he or she is addressing the interpreter as opposed to the client, and allow time afterwards for the interpreter to summarise to the client what has been said.
3) Expect the interpreter to summarise back any exchanges in the client's language, and ask for a summary if this is not offered by the interpreter. This applies to exchanges between interpreter and client or between client and others present.

Pace of the exchange
Interpreting inevitably slows the pace of a conversation. Social workers should therefore:

1) Allow more time for interviews, visits, meetings etc where interpreting takes place.
2) Be prepared to pause at reasonable intervals for interpreting to be done.
3) Be prepared to clarify terminology or difficult concepts in order to help the interpreter to be as accurate as possible.
4) Take full advantage of feedback opportunities to check for misunderstanding.

When the Interpreting Process has ended

The social worker should allow time for discussion with the interpreter. This may cover all or some of the following areas, as appropriate:

1) Assessment and clarification of aspects of the interaction which has taken place.
2) Cultural explanation where appropriate.
3) Feedback in either direction about aspects of the interpreting process.
4) Support and, if necessary, counselling for the interpreter in the case of a particularly distressing interview.

Commentary on the Code

This section amplifies and explains certain parts of the Code.

Basic Responsibility
The limit of this responsibility is of course the point at which the interpreter's responsibility begins. The social worker cannot be responsible for the accuracy of interpretation in a language he or she cannot understand. But the social worker must be responsible for all the other aspects mentioned in the Code.

The Decision to use an Interpreter
This part applies not only where the social worker's parent-tongue is English, but to any situation where social worker and client do not share the same first language.

Emergencies
An emergency is defined as a situation where there is danger to the client, social worker, or the community, or in other circumstances judged to be exceptional in the social worker's professional opinion. It is for the latter to assess the likely consequences of delaying action until an interpreter can be found, as opposed to those of proceeding in circumstances where effective communication cannot take place.

Choice of Interpreter: Use of a client's first language
A social worker who, for example, allows a Panjabi speaking interpreter to 'get by in Hindi' with a Gujarati-speaking client is taking a risk both for him – or herself, and for the client.

The interpreter must be acceptable to both social worker and client
The interpreter may be unacceptable to the client on grounds such as:

Confidentiality: the interpreter may be known to the client.

Gender: there are instances where it may embarrass the client to have an interpreter of the opposite sex – a woman with gynaecological problems may not accept a male interpreter, for example.

Age: a young man in confrontation with his parents over a family matter may not feel comfortable with an older interpreter.

Religion: a woman seeking a divorce may prefer not to have an interpreter of the same religion because she might feel under pressure.

Conflict of interest: the department may be in conflict with the client, and the latter may doubt the ability of a Social Services interpreter to remain impartial.

Confidentiality
The BASW Code of Ethics recognises 'the need to collaborate with others in the interests of clients', but circumscribes this carefully:
'He (the social worker) recognises that information clearly entrusted for one purpose should not be used for another purpose without sanction. He respects the privacy of clients and confidential information about clients gained in his relationship with them or others. He

will divulge such information only with the consent of the client (or informant) except: where there is clear evidence of serious danger to the client, worker, other persons or the community, or in other circumstances, judged exceptional, on the basis of professional consideration and consultation.'

The principle gives the client the final say on whether confidential information should be shared or not, with the exception of emergencies or other exceptional circumstances.

However, the 1983 House of Lords judgement in the case of City of Birmingham District Council v.O. and Another, on the issue of councillors' access to casefiles in an adoption case, introduced what has come to be known as 'the need to know principle'. The Lords came to the following conclusion:

'Bearing in mind that it is the local authority and not the individual social worker which is performing the statutory duty (the social worker is, as it were, the instrument used by the authority) confidential information given to the social worker is given to the authority. However, those who give it are entitled to expect, and social workers can reasonably assure them that, save as may be necessary for the performance of the authority's statutory duties, the information will never be divulged to anyone outside the authority or anyone within the authority who has no need to know.'

This ruling implies that social workers may decide at their own discretion to divulge information to an interpreter if, in their professional opinion, the interpreter has a 'need to know' in order to help them fulfil their statutory obligations.

The practice of *pre-interview briefing* of the interpreter by the social worker is based on the 'need to know' principle.

Form to be signed by Sessional Interpreters

Printed below is is an example of the type of form which should be signed by sessional interpreter employed by a council.

I understand that any information I obtain while interpreting for the Social Services Department of ⎯⎯⎯⎯⎯⎯ Council is confidential.

I will not pass on any such information to anyone without the express permission of the social worker responsible for the client concerned.

I agree to make it known to the Social Services Department if a client is personally known or related to me or if I have any personal interest in the outcome of the interview.

Signed: . . . . (Interpreter)

Address: . . . .

. . . .

Date: . . . . Social Worker: . . . .

Pre-interview briefing – style of interpreting

Most community language interpreters will undertake *consecutive interpreting* – that is, they will wait until the speaker has finished before they begin interpreting. The social worker will therefore need to be aware of the need to pause from time to time during longer pieces of speech, so as to keep the task manageable for the interpreter.

Trained community language interpreting may also be able to undertake a form of *simultaneous interpreting* – that is, interpreting at speed while the conversation is in progress. This is not recommended for one-to-one conversations as it is distracting for the participants. Simultaneous interpreting is however useful in, for instance, court situations where one person does not speak English and needs to be kept in touch with the proceedings without having to interrupt.

Trained interpreters are likely to use *direct interpreting* most of the time – that is, they will speak as if they were the person for whom they are interpreting.

Untrained interpreters are more likely to use *indirect interpreting* – that is, they will preface what they interpret with 'he says' or 'she says'.

When the interpreting process has ended – support

Because they speak the same language as the client, interpreters may be subjected to an emotional barrage during an interview. Interpreters are not trained social workers and may find this an exhausting and disorientating experience. It will be important for social workers involved in such cases to use their own experience of dealing with the stressful side of the job to counsel and support the interpreter. . .

A Code of Practice for Interpreters Working in Social Services Departments

This Code is based on the ethical points taught on the Pathway Diploma course in community language interpreting, but has been focussed specifically on interpreting in the Social Services context. It is intended primarily for permanently employed departmental interpreters, but may be adapted for sessional interpreters.

Why a Code of Practice?

The reasons given in the first four paragraphs of the Code of Practice for social workers apply equally to interpreters working inSocial Services departments, that is:

1) *To protect social work clients*: effective interpreting for clients with limited English will have a crucial bearing on their ability to understand conversations, concepts and processes, voice their own needs, wants and perceptions, and exercise their rights and responsibilities as citizens.

2) *To ensure statutory duties are carried out effectively*: social workers dealing with a client with limited English rely on the interpreter to ensure

96

that statutory duties which require effective communication are carried out.

3) *To protect Social Services staff who use interpreters' services*: social workers who are members of BASW subscribe to a professional code of ethics, and social services staff generally are expected to work to certain professional standards and principles. Because they are unable to understand one side of an interpreted conversation, and have only limited means of checking on the accuracy of what is being conveyed, it is essential for interpreters also to have a set of ethical principles from which to operate. This will also help to build trust between interpreters and those who use their services.

4) *To protect interpreters*: interpreters can encounter difficult ethical decisions in the course of their work, in addition to the inherent responsibility of having to decide how best to convey what is being said. It is essential for them to have a set of guidelines for good practice which will help them resolve ethical prolems if they arise.

The terminology used in the Code is the same as in the Social Workers' Code of Practice. (See p. 90).

Code of Practice

Basic Division of Responsibilities

The interpreter is responsible for facilitating effective communication between social worker and client.

It is for the social worker to decide whether, and how far, the interpreter should be involved, taking into account the client's wishes, the social worker's statutory duties and the need to ensure equality of service delivery.

It is the interpreter's responsibility to advise the social worker about the need for an interpreter, and to draw the social worker's attention to the fact that effective communication is not – or is not likely to – take place, where appropriate.

Choice of Language

In general, an interpreter will interpret best when one of the two languages used is his or her parent-tongue. The interpreter should therefore not agree to interpret from one second language to another *unless* (a) it is an emergency, or (b) alternative interpreters are not available within a reasonable time, and the interpreter has a good level of accuracy and fluency in the second language in question. In such circumstances, the interpreter should make sure that both users know that neither language being used is her or his parent-tongue and establish that this is acceptable before proceeding.

Acceptability of the Interpreter

The interpreter must be acceptable to both social worker and client. The interpreter should therefore check this at the earliest possible stage, so as to avoid delays and embarrassment later.

If the interpreter discovers that a client requiring interpreting is personally known to him or her, or if the interpreter has a personal interest in the outcome of the situation in which interpreting will be undertaken, the interpreter must inform the social worker and, where applicable, the client. It will then be for both users to decide whether or not to proceed. If either does not wish to do so, a different interpreter should be obtained.

Where the department is in conflict with a client and the latter doubts the impartiality of the department's interpreter, the social worker will inform the client that he or she is free to obtain an independent interpreter. In these circumstances the social worker will provide the client with a list of agencies providing the interpreting services, but it will be for the client to make contact with them.

If a client prefers to use his or her own interpreter rather than the department's interpreter, the latter may be asked by the social worker to attend in order to interpret for the social worker and check the accuracy of the client's interpreter.

Confidentiality

Interpreters working as permanent employees of the Social Services department are bound by the same rules of confidentiality as other staff. (For further details see *Commentary* to social workers Code of Practice).

The interpreter should not divulge anything to any person not present during the interpreting process without the express permission of the social worker concerned.

Pre-Interview Briefing

It is essential for the social worker and interpreter to agree the basis on which they will work together before the interpreting process starts. The minimum preparation is outlined in *The Interpreting Process* below. The interpreter should seek the information listed if it is not volunteered by the social worker.

Before the interpreting process starts, the interpreter should set the client at ease by:

1) Introducing him or herself and the social worker.
2) Checking on the language to be used and general acceptability of the interpreter.
3) Explaining how the interview will be conducted and how interpreting will take place.
4) Inviting the client to address the social worker in English (i.e. by-passing the interpreter) at any point if the client has a little English and wishes to do so.

5) Inviting the client to ask for clarification if there is anything he or she does not understand.
6) Reassuring the client about confidentiality if this is felt to be necessary.

The interpreter should warn both users in advance that he or she will interpret everything which is said. This emphasises the interpreters' neutrality and avoids possible embarrassment during the interview.

The Interpreting Process

The interpreter should convey the meaning of everything which is said.

This does not mean literal, word-for-word translation, but it does mean passing on the sense of what is said on both sides without omission. This applies whether the style of interpreting is consecutive or simultaneous.

Users should be encouraged to address each other direct, so as to emphasise that they are the initiators in the conversation, and the interpreter is the intermediary.

If the interpreter summarises then both users must be made aware that this is happening, and secondly both users must agree to it.

Summarising should always be done in indirect speech, to distinguish it from full interpreting, which should always be in the direct form, except where this will lead to misunderstanding.

If the interpreter gives a personal opinion it must be clear to both users that this is taking place and both users must agree to it.

This includes the explanation of cultural differences.

The interpreter must not suggest, through comment, tone of voice or facial expression, that she or he doubts the truth of what has been said. If users contradict themselves in Court it is up to the legal representatives or the magistrate or judge to query it, not the interpreter.

In a less formal situation, the interpreter may point out a contradiction to the user, but only if she or he also informs the other user.

There are special rules governing the conduct of interpreters in police and court situations. (See Chapter 3.) It is the duty of interpreters to familiarise themselves with these and abide by them.

If the interpreter realises that something has not been understood, she or he should explain or clarify briefly. However, if a brief explanation does not solve the problem the matter should be referred back to the originating user for further clarification.

The interpreter has a duty to ensure, as far as possible, that both users understand fully what is going on. This means that brief exchanges between the interpreter and one user (*e.g.* for clarification) should always be summarised for the other user.

Example: 'he asked me what a barrister is and I told him it is a lawyer who can speak for him in court and help him put his case.' This guards against the interpreter giving a wrong explanation.

Requests for clarification addressed by one user to the other user should never be answered by the interpreter. They should always be interpreted so that the user to whom they were addressed can deal with them.

Emotional expression or abusiveness should not be toned down in the interpreted version, unless there is a risk to the physical safety of either the interpreter or one of the users.

A user with limited English who decides to communicate direct with the other user (by-passing the interpreter) should be allowed to do so. The interpreter is there to offer a service. It is for the user to decide whether or not to use it.

The interpreter has a duty to ensure that he or she has understood what has been said before passing it on. This means that the interpreters must ask for clarification if they are not sure if they have understood correctly.

When the Interpreting Process has ended

The interpreter should allow time for discussion with the social worker. This may cover all or some of the following areas, as appropriate:

1) Assessment and clarification of aspects of the interaction which has taken place.
2) Cultural explanation where appropriate.
3) Feedback in either direction about aspects of the interpreting process.

Some social work interviews may be distressing for the interpreter and the latter has the right to seek support and counselling, if required, from the social worker concerned and/or the senior member of staff to whom the interpreter reports.

General Duty to Maintain and Develop Interpreting Skills

Interpreting is a responsible task, and the consequences of misinterpretation can be serious. The interpreter should therefore always try to maintain and develop his or her interpreting skills through learning from practical experience and through attending training courses as appropriate.

Referral and Feedback

Both interpreters and social workers are likely to be out of the office for a good proportion of their time. A written request form as a means of referral between social worker and interpreter can improve efficiency. It also acts as a reminder to social workers that interpreters need to be briefed in advance. The form below was developed by Southall Social Services Area Office, and had an additional function of enabling the office to collect basic information about how the interpreters' services were being used.

Please return to: Interpreting Officer, Social Services, Southall.

REFERRED BY:

Name . . . .   Designation . . . .

Address/Location . . . .   Tel/Ext. No . . . .

. . . .

REFERRED FOR:

Interpreting   ☐

Written Translation   ☐

(Text and instructions should accompany referrals for written translation)

LANGUAGE: Panjabi ☐ Gujerati ☐ Hindi ☐ Urdu ☐

Please indicate where possible:

Date/Time . . . .

Venue . . . .

No. of interviews anticipated   ☐

(Please state if date and time is fixed, or preferred times).

NAME OF CLIENT/FAMILY: . . . .

ADDRESS: . . . .

. . . .

FAMILY DETAILS: (Briefly summarise family composition, current circumstances, and workers involvement)

PURPOSE OF INTERVIEW: (Briefly summarise proposed task of interview for worker and interpreter e.g. interview grandparents to ascertain views re possible R.I.C. of grand-daughter).

Thank you for completing this form – this will assist the interpreter and help in evaluation of the service.

Feedback about interpreting in practice is essential if standards are to be maintained and the service developed. Buckinghamshire County Council devised the two forms below to obtain feedback from sessional interpreters and from staff using their services. This can be of particular value in the case of sessional interpreters, since contact with them is likely to be intermittent. The forms also have the function of encouraging both interpreters and staff to reflect on the interpreting process.

BUCKINGHAMSHIRE COUNTY COUNCIL
SOCIAL SERVICES DEPARTMENT
INTERPRETING SERVICES MONITORING

To be completed by the staff member using the Interpreting Service.

1. Name of Staff member and Area . . . .

    . . . .

2. Name of Interpreter . . . .

3. Language . . . .

4. Date and Time of Session

    Date . . . .

    Time   From . . . . am/pm   To . . . . am/pm

5. Purpose of Session? e.g. assessment, preparation of court report, etc.

6. To what extent did the service help to fulfil that purpose?

7. How happy were you with the role the Interpreter played, bearing in mind accuracy of translation, communication of feeling and mood, etc.?

8. Any other comments?

9. Signed . . . .

BUCKINGHAMSHIRE COUNTY COUNCIL
SOCIAL SERVICES DEPARTMENT
INTERPRETING SERVICES MONITORING

To be completed by Interpreter after each session.

1. Name of Interpreter ....

2. Language ....

3. Staff member and location ....

   ....

4. Date and Length of Session ....

5. What did the Social Worker do to prepare you for the interview?
   e.g. introductory briefing, etc.

6. How happy were you with your role as Interpreter at the interview?

7. Any other comment you would like to make:

8. Signed ....

Please return to the co-ordinator.

Chapter 7

Practice in Community Relations Councils

Introduction

Community Relations Councils (CRCs) have played an important role not only in the early development of English language classes for adults (see Chapter 1) but also in the provision and co-ordination of interpreting. In the sixties and seventies, when interpreting was largely left to the family and friends of those with limited English, CRCs made an important contribution in helping out those who had nobody to interpret for them.

In the eighties, some CRCs began to question whether the direct provision of interpreting services is still an appropriate function for them to perform. There was a growing sense in some areas that statutory bodies should see this as their responsibility and that CRCs' energies would be put to better use in bringing pressure to bear in this respect, rather than continuing to 'do the statutory authorities' job for them'. On the other hand, there was the ever-present demand from individuals in the community for assistance now, and this could put CRCs in a cleft stick when trying to decide how to proceed.

In 1988 Pathway sent questionnaires to all the CRCs in the UK, asking about policy and practice on interpreting. Forty-nine CRCs' replied, providing a 'snapshot' of what half the Community Relations Councils in the country were doing and thinking in relation to this issue. While not comprehensive the survey did provide significant pointers to the state of play.

Forty-four (90%) of the CRCs who responded used the services of interpreters. Three of the five who did not do so had, in fact, only just opened and were not yet fully operational. However, all three expressed concern about interpreting provision.

Most CRCs had access to interpreting facilities for two or more languages, and a third of them had access to interpreting in five languages or more. The frequency with which individual languages were offered reflected the geographical distribution of the sample, and the relative sizes of the ethnic minority populations served.

Table 7.1 The range of languages offered

Number of CRCs offering	Language
29	Urdu
25	Panjabi
23	Hindi
14	Gujarati
14	Bengali
7	Cantonese/Mandarin
3	Vietnamese
3	Arabic
3	Polish
3	Spanish
2	Farsi
2	Italian

Individual CRCs also offered access to interpreting facilities for a wide range of other languages, including Tamil, Somali, Swahili, Turkish, Hungarian, Portuguese, Greek, French, Russian, German, Ukranian. The number of respondents who said they were able to arrange interpreting suggests that the actual list would have certainly been much longer. It was clearly not practical for respondents to list all possibilities.

Community Resources: Strengths and Limitations

None of the CRCs who participated in the survey employed full-time interpreters. Eight employed part-time interpreters, twenty-four used the services of people in the community on a sessional basis, and thirty-one employed bilingual staff who 'helped out' with interpreting as required.

Fifteen CRCs provided interpreting by more than one of the above means.

Sessional Interpreters

Although some of the CRCs using sessional interpreters indicated that this included referrals to local authority, health authority or community interpreting organisations with full or part-time staff, the largest single source of the sessional interpreters used by CRCs were individuals in the community.

Community contacts are a good indication of a CRC's strength, and there is no doubt that some are able to call on a wider range of languages than, say, a local authority interpreting unit or a group of linkworkers in a health authority. Some local authorities have recognised this and made grant aid available to their local CRCs to develop an interpreting service for the area.

Twelve respondents (24%) believed that the CRC was in fact a more appropriate body to provide interpreting services than the local authority. (See Table 7.2). Some of the reasons given are quoted below:

'If the service is based at the CRC but funded by the LA and others it will serve the community better because (a) will benefit from direct feedback (b) won't be fragmented (c) less likely to be perceived as part of the establishment, thus more trusted by the community.' (Hammersmith and Fulham).

'There should be close liaison between CRC and local authorities, CRCs have close contact with local communities and are in touch with their needs. Local authorities should provide funding for paying interpreters.' (Ipswich and Suffolk).

'Due to bureaucratic barriers, the LA units are not easily accessible. In CRC people may just walk in and highlight their need.' (Greenwich).

'CRC has been providing this support for the last 14 years, but it feels that LA should share the responsibilities. So far an adequate service has been provided.' (Tyne and Wear).

Issues of trust, responsiveness and accessibility are uppermost here. Some CRCs clearly feel that a community-based service will be the most effective, and there is a certain weariness about the last of the above comments which probably expresses the feeling of many CRCs that their services have been used for many years by the local authority without any recognition, financial or otherwise, of this fact by the latter.

Other CRCs questioned whether a service provided by the Community Relations Council alone was adequate. Although CRC networks may be able to offer a wider range of languages, they do have the disadvantage that the interpreter is not necessarily easily available. Telephone-calls are not always answered, notes through letter-boxes do not always get a response, and the ability of this kind of system to produce an interpreter on demand will depend, to varying degrees, on whether luck happens to be on the co-ordinator's side.

Bilingual Staff

One response to the above difficulty was to employ bilingual staff, who were able to interpret as and when required in the course of their duties.

Hyndburn and Rossendale CRC went as far as to say:

'We take the view that interpretation is not an ideal to be sought but that service staff should be employed having knowledge of appropriate languages to facilitate effective service delivery direct.'

This CRC, in common with many others, included language ability in the job description of casework staff, who were expected to undertake 'representation and interpretation, and to give advice and guidance on the rights and duties of citizens, so as to assist ethnic minorities 'to adapt to new conditions whilst maintaining a self-respect in their identities and increasing their self-reliance'.

The use of an interpreter will of course always be second-best to the provision of services by workers who are able to switch easily from English to a minority language without needing assistance from a third party. However, Hyndburn and Rossendale CRC did also use CRC members for interpreting 'on an occasional basis' and referred some clients to the local authority-based MSC Community Programme for interpreting services. Although thirty-one (63%) respondents employed bilingual staff, many of them also used sessional interpreters or referred clients elsewhere.

There are a number of reasons why employing bilingual staff is likely to represent part only of the answer to the communication needs of clients from linguistic minorities.

1) Some areas have a very wide range of minority languages (Hammersmith and Fulham CRC quoted 66) and it is unlikely that CRC staffing could ever cover all eventualities.

2) Where language ability is incorporated in a broader job description, it will not always be feasible or efficient to allocate all clients speaking a particular language to a particular member, or members, of staff. The agency may decide, for instance, that a client's need for a representative with a particular area of expertise is greater than the need to be able to communicate directly, when language and expertise do not coincide.

3) There will be situations where it is necessary to separate the advocacy and interpreting roles *e.g.* in court or in other quasi-legal situations.

It is also worth noting that language ability is often 'taken for granted' where bilingual staff are concerned and there is a danger that CRCs will fall into the same trap as many local authorities – of assuming that the ability to interpret derives naturally from the ability to speak a minority language. CRCs employing bilingual staff who have not thought the interpreting function through clearly are even less likely to provide relevant training than those who employ interpreters as such. The result may be frustration among staff and a patchy service to clients.

Part-Time Interpreters

A further response to the problem of availability of sessional interpreters was to employ people specifically as part-time interpreters. In a number of cases provision was funded via the Manpower Services Commission's Community Programme scheme. For example:

1) Warwick CRC employed two part-time interpreters as part of a wider CRC Community Programme consisting of a supervisor and ten support workers.
2) Hounslow CRC employed four part-time interpreters on a similar basis although here there was one local authority funded post.
3) Gwent CRC had three part-time interpreters, who were, however, employed by the Borough Council's CP and 'placed' with the CRC.
4) Medway and Gillingham had two part-time interpreters 'placed' under a similar arrangement with NACRO North Kent CP.

All those we spoke to were concerned about implications of the government's new Employment Training scheme, and whether they would be allowed to continue once the Community Programme scheme was wound up in August 1988. There was also concern about the remit and priorities of the new body, the Training Agency, which replaced the Manpower Services Commission in the same year.

The government's White Paper *Training for Employment* stressed that voluntary organisations who had played an established role in the Community Programme should have the opportunity to contribute to the new scheme. One hundred and seventy thousand project-based places were envisaged for those who had been unemployed for twelve months or more. However, a telephone-call to each of the above schemes a year later found that of the four, only Hounslow CRC was still operating a specific interpreting service, now funded under a borough-linked ET scheme. Clearly it is not possible to generalise from four instances, and there may well have been local factors in the decision to discontinue which had nothing to do with the Training Agency. However, it is only fair to say that we found no evidence – in these instances or elsewhere – or encouragement by the TA to set up or continue interpreting provision through ET. We made several attempts to obtain policy statements from the TA, only to be met with silence or vague replies. No data was available on the number of ET interpreting schemes in the country, and the 1989 guidelines on extra funding available for schemes wanting to help ESOL trainees improve their communication skills made no mention of the need to train participants in interpreting skills. Ironically, the guidelines did suggest that the use of interpreters might help to improve the assessment of prospective ET participants' training needs by monolingual Training Agents, but they failed to address the issue of the training needs of ET-funded interpreters themselves.

This was a sad omission, given the emphasis on vocational training in the White Paper: 'Participants on the new programme will be trainees, not employees' (DE, 1988 para. 5.22). The aim was to provide participants with 'an externally recognised qualification or a credit towards one' (para. 5.18) as well as a record of achievement. The problem appeared to be that the Training Agency had still not recognised bilingualism as a potential vocational asset, and the existence of ET funded interpreting schemes was still not being seen as an opportunity to provide trainees with just the kind of qualification referred to in the White Paper.

Responsibility for the Provision of Interpreting Services

We have already mentioned that just under a quarter of respondents felt that interpreting services were more appropriately provided by the CRC than by the local authority, although there was a strong 'lobby' for LA grant aid for such provision. The complete picture of response is set out below:

Table 7.2

In principle, interpreting services are most appropriately provided by:	No. of CRCs	%
The Community Relations Council	12	24
The Local Authority	13	26
LA and other public services	6	12
Mixed provision (CRC and public services)	13	26
Independent agencies	3	6
None	1	2
Don't know	2	4

The reasons given to support the view that local authorities were the most appropriate providers are summarized by the following comments:

'Under Section 71 of the Race Relations Act 1976, we believe that LA should make fair and equal provision for the whole community. This will mean providing interpretation/translation services where needed.' (Calderdale CRC).

'The LA is the largest service provider in any given area. It is they who ought to provide an interpreting service should it be required.' (Dudley CRC).

'The local authority has the financial resources . . . '(Central Region CRC).

'In Local Authorities the infrastructure exists to recruit, maintain and train interpreters.' (Aylesbury CRC).

'This provides employment on a permanent basis and can ensure that the service is provided when required. It also gives status to minority groups.' (Gwent CRC).

Legal obligation, resources and size were also quoted by those who felt that not only local authorities but other statutory bodies should provide interpreting services. We were surprised that more respondents did not give the reasons advanced by Gwent – that is, accessibility and responsiveness. In principle, the availability of interpreting facilities at

110

the point of service delivery both signals to members of ethnic minority groups that their requirements are recognised and catered for, and also ensures – where interpreters are employed full-time – that the problems of availability are minimised.

Flexibility of provision was identified as an important pre-requisite for effective service delivery by those CRCs which argued for interpreting services to be available from a number of different sources.

> 'Situations vary in different localities. LA should provide the necessary support staff for its own service provision and its clients, but not necessarily for other organisations.' (Ealing CRC).
> 'Statutory agencies should provide their own interpreting services so that those employed become familiar with the situations, terminology and jargon relevant to that agency. CRCs and equivalents should meet their needs and support the voluntary sector.' (Kingston Group for Racial Understanding and Equality).

There was a strong feeling among those respondents that the voluntary and statutory sectors should provide complementary services. CRC provision is not a substitute for statutory authorities accepting their responsibilities for interpreting provision. On the other hand, the existence of such 'statutory' provision does not obviate the need for continuing community provision – for those who prefer to or feel more confident to approach community-based organisations – and to ensure that language resources in the community are fully available, particularly in the case of the communication needs of very small minorities, whose languages are unlikely to be catered for by full-time interpreters. It is also frequently the case that local authority interpreting facilities are only available to members of the public who have business with the authority. For instance, an interpreter based in a Social Services Department may not see it as part of his or her role to accompany a client to a hospital appointment, if this does not involve a social worker or have any direct relation to the department. Some Social Services interpreters would not see it as part of their role to accompany a client to the DHSS, even if the social worker concerned had been giving advice about welfare benefits, on the grounds that DHSS should be making their own interpreting provision. In this kind of situation, a client may have nowhere else to turn but the local CRC.

Co-operation between public authorities and the CRC in this respect would appear to be essential. An example of this was Aylesbury CRE which had worked with Buckinghamshire County Council Social Services Department on the development of a Race Relations Policy for the department, and more recently, the formalisation and extension of the existing network of individuals offering an interpreting service in the community. Lists of sessional interpreters had been drawn up in Milton Keynes, High Wycombe and Aylesbury, following advertisement and interview. Training was to be provided covering social work law, departmental procedures and social work philosophy as well as interpreting techniques. Interpreters were to be paid sessional rates by the department.

The CRC and the local authority agreed that the sessional approach would be most appropriate given the diversity of languages spoken in the area, but the authority recognised the need for co-ordintion and had applied for a post under S.11 in order to ensure that the system was efficient.

A further example of a joint CRC/Local Authority initiative is Strathclyde Interpreting Service which is described in Chapter 5.

Role of CRCs in Identifying Needs

Fifteen of the CRCs surveyed were serving areas where *no statutory body existed to provide an interpreting service of any kind.* A further five served areas where the only provision was by the health authority, usually in the form of Link-workers. In some cases the CRC was able to provide an interpreter through individual contacts, and in others a service was provided by bilingual caseworkers.

Many of these CRCs served areas with substantial linguistic minorities, and it was therefore startling to discover that most of them (seventeen in fact) did not keep any separate record of the demand for language assistance. This proved to be in keeping with the overall picture – thirty-eight (78%) of all the CRCs did not keep figures on numbers of cases dealt with, type of case and languages used, in relation to the demand for interpreting provision. However, we had expected to find CRCs collecting evidence at least in areas where the absence of provision was total.

It is generally accepted that part of the role of CRCs is to identify unmet needs among the ethnic minority communities and draw these to the attention of the relevant authorities. As one CRC put it, 'Service providers should make sure that they comply with legislation with regard to the services of interpreting and translation. The role of the CRC is to make sure this is the case.' Responses to the survey suggested however, that many CRCs were simply meeting needs without collecting the evidence – which was at their fingertips – to make a case for provision by public authorities. Over half of all the CRCs who participated in the survey said they provided interpreting services to local authorities in their area, but only nine of them kept any separate record of the scale and nature of demand.

As we have seen, thirty-four CRCs (69%) stated that they felt interpreting services were most appropriately provided by the local authority, public authorities in general or through mixed provision. (See Table 7.2). Yet twenty-six of these did not keep any separate figures. Thirteen said that they were currently examining the need and/or pressing the local authority to address the issue, but it is difficult to see how they could do this effectively without facts to back up their case. For instance, one of the most frequently cited reasons for not making any public provision is that ethnic minority people are said to prefer family members and friends to interpret. Figures showing the nature and extent of the demand on the CRCs services from individuals with limited English would be a useful way of demonstrating the weakness of this argument.

One possible reason for the lack of data on language need among CRCs is that it is 'taken for granted' as an everyday feature of the offices work. Twenty-two of those CRCs which did not keep figures had bilingual staff who used their language skills on the job. While it is understandable that this attitude should have developed – particularly after years of providing a service – the effect may be to obscure the fact that the CRC is compensating for a gap in statutory provision.

There is, in our view, a pressing need for CRCs to address the issue of monitoring in relation to language need. The fact that four of the eleven who said they were collecting statistics were able to provide them suggests that the others had only recently begun to do so. The figures below, provided by Hammersmith and Fulham CRC Interpreting and Translation Service, provide an example of the way the data can be presented, so as to indicate clusters of demands, in terms of the languages and service sectors concerned. Table 7.3.

Conclusions

Perceptions and attitudes towards interpreting provision and how needs can best be met appear to vary widely between CRCs. The way in which community-based provision developed in the sixties and seventies seems to have led to an unstructured approach often based more on the ad hoc availability of volunteers than on the need to ensure uniform quality of service by the interpreters involved. While there is no doubt that many of the latter have provided, and continue to provide an excellent service, CRCs' informal selection practices and the lack of training suggest that this is not always the case.

There is a growing feeling in some areas that the proper role of a CRC is to put pressure on local and other public authorities to provide interpreters rather than to provide interpreting services itself. Where such a strategy is adopted, then the collection of data on the local demand for interpreters will be crucial. The continuing provision of interpreting services by the CRC can in fact be an important source of such data, at least until alternative provision is available. A rather high proportion of CRCs who replied to the Pathway questionnaire did not seem to monitor demand, even though they usually felt it was an important issue.

In general, CRCs at the end of the eighties seem to have reached a crossroads. The original 'community self-help' approach to interpreting appeared to be giving way to a view that public authorities should be making provision for interpreting needs, but many CRCs seemed unsure of the implications of this shift in perception for their own role. There is certainly a need for more effective information sharing and discussion on the issue, and the Commission for Racial Equality might perform a useful function as facilitator in this respect.

Table 7.3 Interpreting sessions for the period April 1986 to March 1987

Language	Health	DHSS	Education	Social	Legal	Housing	Other	Total
Arabic	25	10	5	6	4	12	4	66
Bengali	86		17	20	1	1	12	137
Chinese			1	2		1		4
Farsi	25	27	1		1	2		56
Greek	3		1	2				6
Portuguese	12	5	8	3	6	4	2	40
Hungarian				2				2
Italian							2	2
Panjabi			1	3		2		6
Polish					1			1
Spanish	3	3		3		4	2	15
Turkish	1			1	3	1		6
Tamil	1					1		2
Urdu	16	4		22	5	7		54
Vietnamese	1		2	1		1		5
Total	173	49	36	65	21	38	20	402

Chapter 8

Education and Training

Introduction

There are clear indications, as outlined in Chapter 2, that language disadvantage is a major contributing factor where low take-up of services exists in multi-racial areas. This, coupled with the legal duty to communicate effectively implied by many of the statutory obligations under which public service organisations operate, suggests that the moment is long overdue for an awareness of the issues highlighted so far to be integrated into both pre- and post-qualification training for social workers and other professionals in the caring services. It also suggests a pressing need for effective training for community language interpreters who work at the interface between ethnic minority groups and statutory bodies. In this chapter we examine the current state of affairs on training both for interpreters and for those using their services, and suggest the directions in which further development could usefully move.

The situation at the end of the eighties gave no cause for complacency. Through Pathway's 1988 survey we were able to establish that fewer than half of the twenty local authorities employing permanent interpreting staff provided any kind of training for interpreters or for social workers using their services. As in the case of sessional interpreters (see Chapter 6) the main reasons for not doing so seemed to be either a lack of awareness of the need for training, or uncertainty about what form training should take, or an apparent absence of local training providers. Coupled with the fact that 70% of authorities using sessional interpreters provided no training for them, these figures gave cause for serious concern.

On the positive side, however, five authorities said that they were planning training for both interpreters and social workers, in addition to those who were already doing something. Training for social workers varied from one to four days in length, with local authorities clearly experimenting in what was for most of them relatively uncharted territory.

Examples of the different types and standards of training for social workers include:

1) 2-day workshop for social workers from Bristol Central area; later to be offered country-wide to all social services staff (Avon C.C.).
2) Joint courses on working together plus inclusion in the approved social worker course (Mental Health) (Bradford MDC).
3) One-day course run by the Race Training Officer (Coventry MDC).
4) 2-day training course for social workers 'Working with Interpreters' (Derbyshire).
5) 4-day course 'Counselling through an Interpreter' (London Borough of Ealing).
6) A 3-day module with one day combined interpreters/users. (Leicestershire C.C).

Later in this chapter we examine the different forms training for social workers in this area could take, including professional training for social work students as well as in-service courses for qualified social workers. It is argued that the 'discrete' and 'integrated' models of social work training for a multi-racial society apply equally well to both groups. Although references are frequently to courses for social workers, many of the points apply equally to other courses for people in the caring professions.

Training for interpreters appeared to represent even more unfamiliar territory. Of the authorities who did provide training, only two had been able to second their interpreters on a course leading to a qualification (Ealing: Pathway Diploma in Community Interpreting; Coventry: Institute of Linguists Bilingual Skills Certificate). It was clear that there was not only a lack of information about such courses, but also a lack of providers in some areas. As a result, what training was provided tended to be more in the nature of induction training than a course which aimed to develop real interpreting skills. However, many of those replying to the Pathway questionnaire requested further information of training leading to validated qualifications.

Training for Interpreters

Background

Professional training for international interpreters has been available for many years. However, the languages offered have tended to be those of the Western industrialised nations, and the opportunity to develop bilingual skills into a vocational asset has, until recently, not been open to speakers of Asian languages in Britain.

Yet interpreting at the community level has been a feature of life in multi-racial areas in Britain for over twenty years – longer in the case of non-Asian ethnic minorities. There has certainly been no shortage of people who might have taken advantage of the chance to obtain a professional interpreting qualification. The Linguistic Minorities Project identified significant numbers of people who were proficient both in English and in a minority language (LMP, 1985, Chapter 5), and in 1974, the PEP survey had already found that a high proportion of Asians with qualifications to 'A'-level standard or above were doing manual jobs. (Smith p.5).

The slowness of Further Education to recognise the potential for vocational training in this area can be attributed to a number of factors.

Firstly, the failure of public authorities to recognise the need to employ their own interpreters meant that even if training has been provided, there would, until recently, have been very few jobs, if any, for newly qualified interpreters. This situation is now changing rapidly and some employers are actively seeking colleges which can provide training for interpreters who are already in post. There is also growing awareness of the need for training for sessional interpreters.

Secondly, the low status afforded until recently to Asian community languages has undoubtedly influenced colleges' thinking. The status of minority languages is generally a function of the socio-economic status of those who speak it. The position of Asians in the labour market, their origins in 'third world' countries with low economic bargaining power, and the reactions of the white community to their presence meant that for many years their ability to communicate in language other than English was seen as an obstacle to 'assimilation' rather than a useful skill. The main response (if any) both in colleges and in schools was to offer ESL teaching. The direct-method approach to teaching ESL was not chosen purely for its methodological merits. It also reflected the fact that, until the mid-eighties, almost all teachers of ESL were mono-lingual whites, and it is only comparatively recently that the gradual increase of bilingual ESL teachers has brought with it a realisation that bilingual teaching methods can be as effective, if not more so. In schools, a similar change in attitude has taken place. Whereas mother-tongue classes for children were almost entirely run by community and religious organisation in the seventies the increase in numers of Asian schoolteachers, accompanied by pressure from the CRE and community groups later resulted in mother-tongue teaching gradually moving away from the temple or mosque – first into lunchtime classes in school and eventually into the mainstream curriculum. Misconceptions about mother-tongue teaching in primary schools 'interfering' with English no longer have much currency and in secondary education GCSEs in some Asian languages are now offered by many schools in multi-racial areas. By the end of the eighties a number of examination boards were also offering Hindi, Panjabi and Urdu 'A'-levels.

Why a Professional Qualification?

There is a widespread misconception among users of interpreters' services that 'if you can speak both languages you can interpret'. In fact, courses which aim to train people for paid employment as interpreters (see below) are over 100 hours. This is because listening for

117

meaning and conveying it accurately, fluently, clearly and at the appropriate speed are skills which have to be learnt and developed over time. The arguments for training which leads to a professional qualification are as follows:

Standards and Responsibility

Interpreting is a responsible task. Both users rely heavily on the interpreter for accurate communication because they cannot understand or check on what is being said in the other language for much of the time. Interpreters are often asked to interpret in legal and quasi-legal situations where important decisions are being made which can have a serious effect on the community user's private life. Training to develop real interpreting skills which are tested under examination conditions means that users have a yardstick for assessing the competence of the interpreter they are using.

There is also a pressing need to give proper recognition to the skills which interpreters have. Interpreters working full-time for local authorities have tended to receive salaries which undervalue their skills, probably because they do not fit easily into job evaluation schemes.

Bilingual staff not employed as interpreters frequently complain that they are pressured into acting as unofficial, unpaid interpreters by white staff who ask them to 'help out'. While few would object to doing this occasionally, we came across instances where the staff concerned felt that their continued co-operation was in fact 'covering up' the real need for the employment of an interpreter. White staff did not recognise the need because they had only a limited concept of what interpreting entailed.

The above points were among the factors which prompted Pathway to develop a qualification for community language interpreters. (described below). Apart from the more obvious aim of establishing professional standards and ethics, the intention was to create a means of validating the skills of community language interpreters so that they would receive due recognition in terms of salary and working relationships, and to reduce the reliance of employers on the *ad hoc* services of their bilingual staff.

Recent and Current Initiations

In 1986 Pathway FE Centre in Southall developed a Diploma in Community Language Interpreting, validated by Ealing College of Higher Education. Since its successful pilot year the course has been offered in Panjabi, Hindi, Urdu, Gujarati, Bengali, Greek, Spanish, Cantonese and Mandarin. The eventual intention is to obtain more general validation so that the Diploma can be offered at various centres in the UK.

In the same year, the Institute of Linguists piloted a Bilingual Skills Certificate at about 'A'-level standard at centres in Manchester,

Burnley, Bedford, Bradford, Accrington and Rossendale and London (Goldsmiths College, Pathway Centre, Clarendon College and Morely College). This certificate is accepted as an appropriate entrance qualification for the Pathway Diploma.

Subsequently, the Institute piloted a certificate in Community Interpreting to provide a follow-on stage to the Bilingual Skills certificate. The standard of this qualification was approximately two years post 'A'-level. This was considered by the Institute to be the minimum possible standard which could produce reliable interpretation, while being within reach of sufficient numbers of people.

Because of time and resource constraints, the Institute's Certificate in Community Interpreting asked participants to specialise in a particular area eg. police and the courts, social services. In 1986 the legal specialisation was provided in Peterborough and Cambridge, producing interpreters to work in Gujarati, Urdu, French, Italian, Spanish, German and Cantonese. The same specialisation was taken in 1987, in Bedford, in Italian, Urdu and Panjabi. The Social Services specialisation was taken in Peterborough in Italian, Gujarati and Bengali.

Whereas the Institute's courses cover both oral and written translation, Pathway's Diploma concentrates almost entirely on oral interpreting (that is, there is no written element in the examination other than the ability to extract information appropriately from a written document and interpret it.) This enables trainees to acquire, over the same length of time, a high level of general competency in oral skills so as to be able to operate with maximum flexibility in a variety of contexts. A separate Diploma in Translation is being developed, in order to be able to meet employers' requirements for a translation qualification while doing justice to the very different skills which translation involves.

Oral interpreting requires extremely good listening skills, immediate recall, and an ability to convert meaning from one language to another on the spot, while related to both users and controlling the process as necessary. Written translation, onthe other hand, requires the more reflective capacity to deduce meaning taking into account the writer's intention and the context. Translation takes place at a different pace so that nuances of meaning, style and readability can be given full attention. Face to face interaction is not central to the activity, as it is in the case of oral interpreting, but an understanding of the reader's viewpoint and potential difficulties is essential. Although there is an overlap between the two disciplines, there is in Pathway's view sufficient difference between the skills required to justify separate courses and separate qualifications.

Pathway's Diploma in Community Language Interpreting is taught over one hundred and twenty hours and includes twenty-one hours placement with a public service agency. The areas covered are as follows:

Spoken language skills: Trainees must attain a high degree of accuracy, clarity, fluency and speed, in English and the chosen Asian language.

Process skills: Trainees must be able to:

1) Establish an effective working relationship with both users before beginning the interview.
2) Use direct and indirect interpreting appropriately.
3) Check and clarify meaning as appropriate.
4) Control the speed and quantity of information to be interpreted.
5) Keep both users in touch with the proceedings throughout.
6) Deal effectively with unpredictables (*e.g.* an aggressive or tearful user).
7) Switch appropriately from one language to the other.

Both language and process skills are tested by role-played interviews where the interpreters must demonstrate their abilities in practice.

Agency knowledge: In addition trainees are briefed on public institutions – social services and other local authority and government departments, the health service, police and courts. Trainees are tested on this in an interview at the end of the course.

Ethics: The interpreter is constantly making decisions about meaning and emphasis. In addition he/she may have to take decisions about when to intervene and how. These aspects of the interpreter's job have ethical implications which are explored in detail during training. Trainees' understanding of a Code of Ethics is developed during the course and trainees are tested on this in a final interview.

In addition to the above initiatives, a number of shorter courses have appeared over the last few years. They aim to provide participants with a basic familiarisation with the role and skills of the interpreter, and often act as 'feeders' to the longer certificated courses. Southall College of Technology for instance, runs a ten week (thirty hours) introductory course in community interpreting in Asian languages. Another example is the London Interpreting Project which runs twelve week courses for members of the Latin American, Italian and Turkish communities, who want to prepare for the Bilingual Skills Certificate. Pathway has also developed a short intensive (four day) introductory course for sessional interpreters. The first of these courses was devised in response to a request from Harlow Council in 1989.

The recent nature of most of these initiatives means that there are, as yet, comparatively few professionally qualified community interpreters who speak Asian languages. However, it is anticipated that the current developments described will radically change the balance between trained and untrained interpreters among those offering their services to social workers over the next few years. It will be important for prospective employers to be aware of the professional qualifications which exist, and take account of them during the selection process. It will be equally important for employers to be aware of the benefits of seconding unqualified staff for this kind of training.

Training for Staff in Working Through an Interpreter

Background

The latter half of the eighties has seen a substantial increase in the number of race-related training initiatives undertaken in local authorities, often, but not always, linked with the adoption of an equal opportunity policy by the Council concerned. This has coincided with a growing awareness of the importance of addressing race-related issues among providers of social work training. The conditions set by the Central Council for Education and Training in Social Work (CCETSW) for validation of courses leading to professional social work qualifications now include a requirement to train students for work in a multi-racial society in practice as well as theory. The Council's working paper 'Teaching Social Work for a Multi-Racial Society' pointed out that approaches to training on race-related issues on courses leading to the Certificate of Qualification in Social Work (CQSW) generally fell into one of the following categories:

Discrete teaching: courses, workshops, devoted specifically to topics related to ethnic minorities.

Integrated teaching: the incorporation of material related to ethnic minorities into core courses such as psychology, sociology, social policy, law and social work theory, and into the teaching of social work practice.

The advantage of the integrated approach is that the presence of ethnic minorities in Britain and the development of a multi-racial society are taken as fundamental to the course as a whole, because they are built into the mainstream curriculum, rather than being 'tacked on' as a specialist, often optional subject. However, reliance on this approach alone can mean that particular aspects which need separate attention in order to develop specific skills and understanding are lost. The integrated model does not easily allow students to develop detailed knowledge or practical ability in areas such as fostering services and the black communities, the needs of ethnic minority elderly people, or cultural factors in mental illness.

The authors share CCETSW's view that the two models complement each other and should both, ideally, be built into training for those working in the caring services in multi-racial areas – whether for students or for qualified staff undergoing in-service training. The application of the two models to interpreter-related training for each of these groups is set out below:

Discrete Teaching:

The skills of working through an interpreter can only be effectively acquired through practical role-plays with non-English speaking clients, in which students can learn to use the interpreting process effectively at first hand. The involvement of practising interpreters in such exercises is essential – preferably these should be interpreters with experience of situations relevant to the public service concerned. Ethnically mixed student groups provide opportunities for bilingual students to experience the role of interpreter and client, and for monolingual students to experience what it feels like to be a second language speaking client through exercises where the roles are reversed. Such groups also provide the trainer with an opportunity to establish and validate bilingualism as a skill, and to explore the respective roles of interpreter and bilingual social worker.

We would argue that the importance of effective communication in enabling the social worker to fulfil his or her legal obligations is such that practical training in the skills of working through an interpreter should be an essential part of every course leading to a professional social work qualification. To leave it out or include it as an option only is to invite repetitions of the Birmingham case (see Chapter three). All students should be familiar with Codes of Practice such as those included in Chapter 6.

Integrated Teaching:

Trainers and lecturers on professional courses in the caring fields who want to develop a truly integrated approach to teaching in a multi-racial society will find many occasions to incorporate and refer to the links between language, culture and ethnicity on the one hand, and discrimination and disadvantage on the other. For example:

1) Social policy and administration courses should include discussion of the response of central and local government to the development of black linguistic minority communities in Britain (see chapter 1).

2) Teaching on community structures, migration and social history should include detail on the languages, and experience of ethnic minority groups.

3) Sociology and economics courses which focus on inequality should pay specific attention to the effects of language disadvantage (see Chapter 2).

4) Teaching on welfare benefits and take-up of services should clearly identify language as a contributory factor to low take-up and examine the possible solutions (see Chapter 2).

5) Teaching on legal aspects of social work should stress the social workers' duty to communicate effectively in order to comply with the law (see Chapter 3).

6) Teaching on the family should include exploration of the dynamics of situations where levels of English vary between family members, and the implications of this for family relationships and for social work practice.

7) Discussion of the casework relationship should include analysis of the 'white social worker – black client' dynamic, and the effect of

introducing an interpreter. It should also include an exploration of bilingual social work and clarify the respective roles of bilingual social worker and interpreter.

8) Training in counselling, interviewing skills and court work should include work with an interpreter.

9) Student projects and placements involving work with black community organisations should focus clearly on the language dimension.

The extent to which these kind of connections are made will depend very much on the extent to which training establishments are successful in increasing their proportions of black bilingual students and staff. CCETSW's 1985 study, *Ethnic Minorities and Social Work Training*, found that although numbers of ethnic minority CQSW students were rising, much of the increase was accounted for by Afro-Caribbean women (CCETSW, 1985 Table 5). The proportions of Asians remain low, as do the proportions of Asian staff in establishments providing training. The CCETSW working paper stressed that the integrated approach relies heavily for its success on the combined efforts of a staff group convinced of its value. 'Otherwise integrated teaching may only be nominal, involving little more than relevant books on a reading list of superficial illustrative references' (p.21). It is for the white majority of teachers on professional courses to demonstrate that the integrated approach is more than a token gesture.

Problems and Difficulties with Discrete Teaching

Experienced staff tend to become impatient with training which appears over-academic and out of touch with the realities of their everyday work. Training for work with an interpreter should therefore concentrate primarily on the development of practical skills and the resolution of real problems which participants have already encountered in their work.

Participants on two four-day workshops run by Pathway for LB Ealing Social Services were asked, at the start of the first day, to say what they wanted out of the course. Without exception, their expectations were closely linked to practical difficulties encountered in their work:

1) Basic information about Asian languages, religions, names re. choosing the right interpreter for the client.

2) Wanting to feel more 'comfortable' using the services of an interpreter. What is the right way to get the information I need?

3) Being able to trust the interpreter: is what I or the client is saying being censored?

4) How to deal with the feeling of 'being shut out': client seems to relate more to the interpreter than to me.

5) Roles: who is in control of the interview? Who should take the initiative if the client appears to be rambling? Or if the client bursts into tears?

6) Using the interpreter with sensitivity: am I over-controlling? Not letting the interpreter in?
7) How to judge if the way I am communicating is right for the interpreter – especially in relation to difficult concepts, explaining policy in terms to which clients can relate.
8) The interpreter's role in assessing the need for an interpreter in the first place – who decides?
9) Role of the interpreter in planning visits and assessment afterwards
10) Use of interpreter for cultural knowledge as well as simply language skills.
11) How to work through an interpreter in family group situations where individuals have different levels of competence in English.

In-service courses in working through an interpreter should include 'first line' staff such as receptionists as well as professionally qualified staff, since the former are often the first point of contact between the organisation and the client with limited English. Their assessment of the need for an interpreter and the way they handle the interaction with the client can be very important in determining the extent to which equality of service is maintained.

Process Skills

If participants are to develop real skills, as opposed to simply a faint increase in awareness, then the course will need to be three or four days in length. The process skills to be covered will include the ability to:

1) Decide when an interpreter is necessary.
2) Establish enough information about a client with little English to be able to contact the appropriate interpreter.
3) Deal efficiently with situations where the client has brought his/her own (untrained interpreter – often a close relative).
4) Brief the interpreter effectively before an interview or home visit.
5) Establish a shared understanding with the interpreter of the purpose of the interview, the respective roles of officer and interpreter, and the process plan.
6) Use the non-verbal dynamics of the interpreting situation effectively.
7) Control their own communication in terms of quantity, complexity of thought and language, and style of delivery, in such a way as to be as helpful as possible to the interpreter.
8) Check and question the interpreting being done sensitively without undermining the interpreting process.
9) Use constructively the 'thinking space' generated in an interpreted interview as a result of the slowed pace.
10) Create a relationship with the client through and apart from the interpreter.
11) Ensure the client is not intimidated or frustrated by the interpreting process.

12) Respond helpfully to interpreters' difficulties, especially requests for clarification or repetition.
13) Maintain control of the interview while allowing interpreter interventions where appropriate.
14) Give the interpreter process instructions (*e.g.* an 'aside' re. how to put a particular question).
15) Use the developing relationship between interpreter and client during a series of visits.
16) Work with an interpreter in formal situations (*e.g.* court, case conference.)
17) Use the interpreter's skills in non-language areas such as cultural explanation.

The above skills should be applied to situations involving

1) Single clients.
2) Two clients, or client with relative or friend.
3) Family groups where all members have limited English.
4) Family groups where only some members have limited English.

Although the primary focus of such a course should be process skills, the training is also likely to involve the acquisition of new knowledge and, equally important, a re-examination of professional attitudes as the relationship with the interpreter and with the client are explored.

Knowledge

Participants should develop understanding in the following areas:

1) The relevance of good interpreting to professional and statutory objectives and quality of service to black clients.
2) The role of interpreters and when and how to use them.
3) The dynamics of the interpreting situation and the ways in which the social worker can help or hinder the interpreting process.
4) The different interpreting techniques and their uses.
5) The linguistic and ethical decisions interpreters have to make.
6) The pressures interpreters may be under and the need for briefing and de-briefing.
7) Basic background knowledge of Asian languages in countries of origin and UK, and the connection with religions and the local community (particularly re. appropriate choice of interpreter).
8) The contribution the interpreter is able to make in non-language areas such as cultural explanation.

Attitudes

Participants should develop:

1) Expectations of an interview through an interpreter which are as high as their expectations of the average interview with a white English client.

2) Empathy with the client's position in an interpreted interview, and an awareness of the danger of the client slipping into a passive role or becoming frustrated.
3) Readiness to respond helpfully to the interpreters' difficulties, especially to requests for clarification or repetition.
4) Readiness to control their own communication in terms of quantity, complexity of thought and language, and style of delivery in such a way as to be as helpful as possible to the interpreter.
5) Readiness to treat the trained interpreter as a skilled professional, who can advise the Social Worker on effective communication.
6) Readiness to use the interpreters' skills in non-language areas, such as cultural explanation.
7) Readiness to trust the in-house interpreter with confidential information where this is necessary to prepare him or her adequately.
8) Readiness to work with the interpreter as an equal, sharing the objectives of the interview in advance and discussing the process before and after an interview.

Problems and Difficulties with Integrated Teaching

Specific courses on working through an interpreter need to be reinforced by the integration of the language dimension into in-service courses in general, in particular, those dealing with statutory duties.

An example is the content of courses for those seeking approval under the Mental Health Act. CCETSW's objectives for such courses state that participants should obtain, inter alia:

1) Knowledge and understanding of the nature of mental disorder and its treatment, in family, social, cultural and ethnic contexts.
2) Knowledge and use of appropriate local resources and community networks, and of statutory, voluntary and private resources for the care, treatment and support of clients/patients and their relatives. (CCETSW, 1987 p.6).

The core elements of the curriculum of such courses include:

1) Appropriate communication through interviews and/or discussion with patients, relatives.
2) The influence of social, ethnic, cultural background and/or religious belief as it might affect the expression of disturbance disorder or impairment, which might also create difficulties in communication with clients/patients and their relatives, friends, etc.
3) Understanding of language/communication difficulties, handicapping conditions, discrimination on the basis of sex, age, class, ethnic origin, etc. (CCETSW, 1987 pp. 9–11).

These objectives and core elements imply, at the very least, a knowledge of when and where to involve an interpreter. In our view they suggest a need for practical skills development in how to work effectively through an interpreter in the often complex circumstances encountered in mental health situations. It is disappointing to find that CCETSW's suggestions for appropriate teaching methods and learning opportunities do not include any mention of practical communication exercises or the activation of case-studies through role-plays using an interpreter. This is an omission which needs to be addressed.

Other opportunities for the integration of communication and interpreting material include:

1) Courses on child abuse prevention and emergency provisions.
2) Courses dealing with care of the elderly and placing of clients in residential care.
3) Courses on child offenders and juvenile court work, where relatives do not speak English.

If the approach on such courses is to ignore the communication dimension, then discrete courses on working through an interpreter are likely to be marginalised, and the benefit to ethnic minority clients drastically reduced. We have already argued that interpreting provision should be seen as part of the mainstream of a local authority's equal opportunity policy, if it is to be effective. The same applies to interpreter-linked training.

Public service training officers will need to use their bargaining power as purchasers of training from outside agencies to ask questions about the inclusion of language disadvantage in course content. Where they themselves run the training they will be well-placed to make changes where required.

Conclusions

Training for community language interpreters has already 'taken off' with the Pathway and Institute of Linguists initiatives. There is no shortage of staff in colleges of Further and Higher Education with language teaching qualifications – even with experience of training interpreters. However, bilingual staff with the relevant experience and qualifications to teach community language interpreting – as opposed to European languages – may be harder to find. The best starting point for managers in public services who want to train full-time or sessional interpreters is to approach local colleges and ask them to devise a course. The colleges may well have the staff – or at least some of the staff – and may be able to put together a course team who jointly make up the skills required. Back-up advice can be obtained either from Pathway or from the Institute of Linguists. This is a new field which is developing fast, and fresh possibilities are continually emerging.

There is now an urgent need for a formally established professional body of community language interpreters, which can set standards, encourage the development of training and monitor provision.

We have argued that the ability to work effectively through an interpreter is an essential skill for professionals and 'front-line' staff serving multi-racial areas. Training in these skills should be integrated into both pre- and post-qualifying courses. The accumulating evidence that language disadvantage is associated with other forms of deprivation should also be integrated into the basic materials of professional training courses. Until this has been achieved, there will be a continuing need for specific short courses on working through an interpreter, so that staff in public services can ensure that they are providing a fair service, regardless of the clients' linguistic ability.

Chapter 9

Pointers Towards the Next Steps in Policy Development

First Steps

Since the 1976 Race Relations Act there has been a marked increase in the number of local authorities with formal equal opportunity policies. This has, in some cases, resulted in closer attention being paid to the needs of ethnic minority clients in the planning of services. There is a growing recognition of the link between staffing policy and the effectiveness of service delivery to minority communities, which is leading to the appointment both of ethnic minority social workers and interpreters.

The fact of having a formal equal opportunity policy does not, however, automatically lead to greater responsiveness. All the local authorities who responded to Pathway's questionnaire had such a policy, but there was considerable variation in the extent to which they had examined needs and issues relating to ethnic minority 'consumers' of services. A significant proportion of those already employing interpreters had drawn up a departmental race equality policy and plan, and our research suggests that the process of drawing up departmental plans is likely to alert managers to unmet needs for interpreting provision.

The adoption of an equal opportunities policy is clearly an important first step, but it is the implementation of the policy which brings it alive, and ensures that it is not simply a piece of paper.

A Basis for Policy

It is difficult to identify need and respond to it if the facts of the local situation are not available. Although the large studies quoted in this book give clear indications of links between language disadvantage and other forms of deprivation from a national perspective, it will nevertheless often be necessary for a local case to be made, in order to justify expenditure on interpreting.

Although our research identified a clear trend towards monitoring the ethnic origins of staff, monitoring of clients' ethnic origin, while on the increase, remained much less widespread. Public bodies with a genuine desire to establish the extent to which language may be a factor in the take-up or effectiveness of services will need to introduce methods for monitoring clients; ethnic origin – and interpreting the data obtained.

Many local authorities are already using sessional interpreters, some on a largely *ad hoc* basis, others through a co-ordinated register. We have noted that the nature and extent of demand for sessional interpreting can in itself provide a good indicator of need, (provided, of course, the availability of sessionals is publicised effectively to potential users). It was therefore disappointing to find that record-keeping in relation to interpreting provision was not usually comprehensive in coverage nor, with some exceptions, was it collated in a meaningful way. Most of the authorities who did keep records were able to account for the number of requests met and which language had been used, but requests from social workers were recorded more frequently than those from clients. This form of recording may obscure instances where social workers or receptionists are refusing or 'filtering out' requests for an interpreter, or where an interpreting service is over-stretched and a certain amount of 'rationing' is going on.

It is important to keep a record of the type of case for which an interpreter is needed so that the departments can establish the extent to which statutory functions are affected by communication difficulties, as well as collecting information about the nature of the work which may help in recruitment and training decisions, for both interpreters and social workers.

It was of particular concern that a number of local authorities with Section 11 funded interpreting posts kept inadequate records – an unsatisfactory state of affairs, given the Home Office requirement for authorities to be able to account for the work undertaken by Section 11 postholders. Also, over 60% of participating authorities kept no reords at all of their interpreting provision, thereby depriving policy-makers of an indicator of the extent of the need.

For the future, clear indicators of language disadvantage will be essential if this important area is to be addressed adequately at local level. In this context, it was disappointing to find that more than three-quarters of all Community Relations Councils surveyed did not keep any records of demand and supply in relation to their interpreting provision. It would appear that many CRCs were simply meeting needs without collecting the evidence – which is at their fingertips – to make a case for provision by public authorities. This lack of data is inconsistent with CRCs' role in identifying local needs and pressing for appropriate mainstream provision.

In fact, perceptions and attitudes related to interpreting provision and how language needs could best be met varied widely betweeen CRCs, and there appeared to be a need for more effective information sharing and discussion on the subject. Perhaps the Commission for Racial Equality could facilitate such a process?

Accepting Responsibility

There has been a significant shift in attitudes among local authorities, on the question 'who should be responsible for providing an interpreter?' Whereas the general view in the sixties and seventies was that individual clients should make their own arrangements through informal contacts in the community, the eighties have seen a gradual change of attitude.

70% of all Social Services departments who responded to Pathway's questionnaire felt that interpreters should be provided by the local authority. Just over a third of these felt that other statutory bodies should also provide interpreting services, so that the facility was available at whatever point it was needed. This view is complemented by the fact that almost all the clients interviewed by Pathway said they would prefer to use a trained interpreter employed by the Social Services department rather than family or friends.

52% of Community Relations Councils felt that interpreting services were most appropriately provided by either the local authority or by a combination of CRC and public services. 24% felt that the CRC alone was the most appropriate provider, reflecting in part the fact that CRCs have grown accustomed to providing interpreting in the absence of provision by local authorities – and now see it as part of their role – and in part a feeling that CRCs were more responsive and accessible to the ethnic minority community, and therefore more likely to be trusted and effective, than local authority departments.

Accessibility and availability are important in the social context – particularly when dealing with crises. Duty social workers should be able to call on a duty interpreter. It is clearly not effective to have to ask a client who is depressed and considering suicide to 'come back tomorrow when we've found an interpreter'.

On the other hand it is likely that some individuals might prefer to approach the CRC, and there is also the fact that local authority-based interpreters are often only able to assist those who have business with the Council, and may have to turn away individuals who, for instance, want an interpreter to accompany them to court or to the DHSS.

In our view, community-based and local authority interpreting provision should be seen as complementary. The former is no substitute for the latter, if clients' needs are to be adequately met, and statutory duties are to be fulfilled. But, equally, the employment of interpreters by the local authority should not be seen as removing the need for a community-based service.

In principle, public service bodies serving multi-racial communities with a significant proportion of people speaking languages other than English should employ full-time interpreter(s) to cover the main minority language(s) spoken, in order to ensure maximum availability and accessibility at the point of service delivery. In addition a register of sessional interpreters should be developed to cover languages spoken by less numerous groups and co-ordinated either by the full-time interpreter(s) – or by a local community organisation (by agreement).

Where an arrangement of this kind is made with a community organisation, financial support should be considered if the public body using the service wants to make sure that sessional interpreters are effectively selected and trained.

Clearly, the exact form which interpreting provision takes will vary according to local needs, but it is now widely accepted that 'leaving it to the client to organise' is no longer an appropriate policy – if it ever was.

Standards

As we have seen, just over three quarters of the local authorities participating in the survey used the services of sessional interpreters. It was disturbing to discover that just under two thirds of these had no formal selection procedures for sessional interpreters. Where the latter were supplied by a Community Relations Council or voluntary or religious organisation it appeared to be assumed that they would have been 'vetted' by the body concerned. In fact, the results of Pathway's CRC survey suggest that they are likely to have been recruited in a very informal manner. The same would apply to other voluntary organisations in many cases.

Those local authorities who did have a formal selection process for sessional interpreters generally limited themselves to an interview carried out in English and another language. While this is a step in the right direction, a conversation carried out in an Asian language is not a test of interpreting ability, only of fluency in the language concerned. Only four authorities conducted a test of interpreting ability separately from the interview.

We would recommend that any public body using interpreters whether full-time, part-time or sessional – should develop proper selection processes, in order to ensure that the quality of interpreting is of a standard which fulfils professional and statutory obligations and meets clients' needs.

The *ad hoc* use of bilingual staff as interpreters, where this is not part of their job description, and where no financial recognition is given for this service, has the following inherent dangers:

1) Although fluent in both languages, they are unlikely to have been trained to interpret.
2) The skills involved are often taken for granted by mono-lingual staff. Bilingual staff may withdraw their goodwill if demands on their services become excessive.
3) The nature and extent to which their services are used is rarely monitored, and they may, in fact, be covering up the real need for an interpreter to be employed.

132

On the other hand, it is clearly important for public bodies to employ bilingual staff where a significant proportion of users of the service speak a language other than English. Employers will need to be clear whether they are employing a bilingual person primarily for their professional skills (*e.g.* as social worker, housing officer, nurse), or because they can communicate in a language other than English. If the latter aspect is a significant factor, then it will need to be written into the employee's job description and treated as a skill which can be assessed through job evaluation. Job descriptions should make clear whether such employees are only expected to use their language skills with their own clients, or whether they are also expected to interpret for colleagues.

If interpreting is required, then we would recommend both an interpreting aptitude test at the selection stage and a short course in basic interpreting skills as soon as possible after appointment.

Interpreting between social worker and client is a task which carries considerable responsibility, given the personal implications for the client and the legal and professional framework within which the social worker operates. It is important for roles to be clearly defined, and for the context in which ethical decisions have to be made to be clearly understood by all three. Public service organisations using interpreters will need to develop locally relevant Codes of Practice for both interpreters and provide training for staff in the Codes' implications for their day-to-day work.

Training

Training for community language interpreters is developing rapidly. Longer courses such as Pathway's Diploma in Community Interpreting or the Institute of Linguists' Certificate are becoming more widely available, and there is also increasing numbers of shorter introductory courses.

Public bodies wanting training for interpreters may find it useful to initiate discussions with local FE or HE providers of language and communication courses, who may be ready to develop locally relevant tuition. Alternatively, advice and assistance are available from either Pathway or the Institute.

We have noted that some of the CRCs surveyed employed interpreters through the Community Programme scheme funded by the Manpower Services Commission. A few CRCs have since been able to provide an interpreting service through the Employment Training Scheme funded by MSC's successor the Training Agency. Unfortunately, the administration of both CP and ET has been dogged by a lack of clear policy at government level on the training of interpreters funded in this way – in spite of the emphasis placed on the need to ensure that such schemes provide vocational training. There is a pressing need for the Training Agency to review the situation in the light of the job opportunities being opened up by the importance now being given to interpreting by public service employers.

Apart from training interpreters, it will be important for employers also to provide training for those monolingual staff who need to work through them. Courses may range from two to four days, depending on the level of competence required. One-day 'awareness' courses are also available. Pathway can provide advice and assistance in this area.

It will also be important for the same skills and awareness to be integrated into professional training for 'customer-contact' staff in general. This includes pre-qualification courses such as the CQSW, and post-qualifying courses such as those for social workers seeking approval under the Mental Health Act.

A growing need

We have found strong indications that public service bodies are likely to be faced with increasing demand from clients with limited English as a result of the link between language disadvantage and other factors, such as:

1) Greater vulnerability to redundancy among black people with limited English, as a result of being employed in older, more labour-intensive, less skilled occupations which are increasingly likely to be subject to rationalisation. Their difficulties in obtaining a job following redundancy is undoubtedly a contributing factor to the higher than average unemployment rate among black people.
2) The growing number of ethnic minority pensioners, many of whom have not been able to learn English during their working lives.
3) The fact that people with limited English are more likely to have below average earnings and to live in sub-standard housing.
4) A growing body of evidence indicating a link between communication difficulties and low take-up benefits and services.

There is a need for:

1) Public service providers to recognise people with limited English as an identifiable group within the community who are likely to be particularly in need of support.
2) Further research to be undertaken on the link between communication difficulties and low take-up benefits and services. This has been impeded in the past by the lack of data on clients' ethnic origin, but the trend towards ethnic monitoring among local authorities should make it feasible in the future.
3) Specific research to be undertaken on ethnic minority clients' perceptions of Social Services departments (and of their social workers). The studies which exist so far relate only to the perceptions of white clients.

It is important for local authorities to link the identification of language deprivation in the community not only with interpreting provision, but also with the provision of English classes for adults, an area of public policy which has been consistently under-funded by central government. One of the main changes of attitude and perception which has occurred since the sixties is that interpreting and language tuition are complementary, rather than mutually exclusive areas of policy.

The mounting evidence of a link between limited English and other forms of disadvantage led the House of Commons Affairs Committee to describe the unsatisfactory nature of ESL provision as 'a matter of national importance'. (1986, see Chapter 1).

Since then some additional provision for ESL for unemployed people has been made through the Employment Training Scheme, but funding of the national Industrial Language Training Scheme has been terminated, resulting in closure of many local Units. ILT represented the only national provision for teaching English and communication in the workplace, and the loss of over £2 million in resources in this area has left a yawning gap. There is an urgent need for a comprehensive review of ESL provision nationally so that a real strategy can be devised, based on a realistic assessment of needs.

The unsatisfactory nature of the current situation only serves to underline the need for interpreting provision.

Genuine commitment

Finally, we would like to stress how important it is for any public service employing interpreters to be clear about why this is being done, and how this fits into the authority's wider equal opportunities strategy. The appointment of interpreters can be a functional adjunct to an overall policy of employing representative proportions of black staff (including bilingual staff) or it can be an excuse of continuing to employ mostly white staff, in spite of the existence of a substantial black clientele. The decision to look at interpreting provision as an issue may itself have been provoked by the consequences of recruitment and training policies which had led to very few black staff being appointed. To employ interpreters without also addressing this basic issue would look very much like 'papering over the cracks.' Public services considering the employment of interpreters should therefore do this in the context of an overall review of the relationship between staffing and service delivery to members of ethnic and linguistic minorities.

Bibliography

ADSS/CRE 1978: 'Multi-racial Britain, the Social Services Response'. Commission for Racial Equality and Association of Directors of Social Services.

ADSS 1982: 'Social Services and Ethnic Minorities'. Report of a questionnaire survey. Association of Directors of Social Services.

ALA 1988: 'Black People, Ethnic Minorities and the Poll Tax'. Association of London Authorities.

ALBSU/RRL 1989: 'Communication Skills among Non English First Language Speakers'. Adult Literacy and Basic Skills Unit and Research Resources Ltd.

BASW 1982: 'Social Work in Multi-Cultural Britain – Guidelines for Preparation and Practice'. British Association of Social Workers.

BASW 1983: 'The Mental Health Act 1983 – A Guide for Social Workers.'

BASW 1985 'A Code of Ethics for Social Work' Ed. David Watson. RKP.

BASW 1987: Paper by Social Work and Racism Group, Birmingham and Solihull BASW branch.

BROWN 1983: 'The Approved Social Workers Guide to the Mental Health Act 1983' Community Care.

CANNAN 1983: 'Social Work, Race Relations and the Social Work Curriculum' Crescy Cannan in 'New Community' Vol XI, Nos 1/2. Commission for Racial Equality.

CCETSW 1983: 'Teaching Social Work for a Multi-Racial Society' Report of a Working Group of the Central Council for Education and Training in Social Work. Paper 21.

CCETSW 1985: 'Ethnic Minorities and Social Work Training' Paper 21.1

CCETSW 1987: 'Regulations and Guidance for the Training of Social Workers to be considered for approval in England and Wales under the Mental Health Act 1983'. Paper 19.19.

CHANNAN 1982: 'The Role of the Court Interpreter'. Omkar Nath Channan. Pub. Shaw & Sons.

CHEETHAM 1981: 'Social Work Services for Ethnic Minorities in Britain and the U.S.A'. Juliet Cheetham.

CHEETHAM 1982: 'Social Work and Ethnicity' Ed. Juliet-Cheetham. Pub. George Allen & Unwin.

CLAIBORNE 1974: 'Race and Law in Britain and the United States'. Minority Rights Group Report, No. 22.

CMND 2739: 'Immigration from the Commonwealth' White Paper 1965.

CMND 8476: 'The Government Reply to the Home Affairs Committee Report on Racial Disadvantage'. HMSO. 1981.

CONNELLY N. 1981: 'Social Services Provision in Multi-Racial Area'. Policy Studies Institute.

CPAG 1985: 'Passport to Benefits?! Racism in Social Security' P. Gordon and A. Newnham. Child Poverty Action Group.

CRC 1973: Community Relations Commission. Reprint from 'Education and Community Relations'. (CRC ED B.0127).

CRC 1977: 'Urban Deprivation, Racial Inequality and Social Policy': A report, Community Relations Commission (now CRE).

CRE/NCILT 1978: 'The Language Barrier in Employment'. Fact paper No. 4. Commission for Racial Equality.

CRE 1980: 'Racial Equality and Social Policies in London'. A discussion paper presented by the CRE to the London Boroughs Association.

CRE 1984: 'Race and Council Housing in Hackney: Report of a formal investigation'. Commission for Racial Equality.

CRE 1985: 'Review of the Race Relations Act 1976: Proposals for change'. Commission for Racial Equality.

DE 1988: 'Training for Employment' CM 316 Department of Employment. HMSO.

DOE 1983: 'Local Authorities and Racial Disadvantage'. Report of a joint Government/Local Authority Association Working Group. Department of the Environment. HMSO.

ELY P. and DENNEY D. 1987: 'Social Work in a Multi-racial Society'. Gower.

FITZGERALD M. 1985: 'Section 71 of the Race Relations Act 1976. A case study' CRE.

FRYER P. 1984: 'Staying Power'. Pluto.

GR 1987: 'The Government Reply to the First Report from the Home Affairs Committee'. CM 193. HMSO.

HAC 1981: 'Racial Disadvantage. Fifth Report of the House of Commons Home Affairs Committee'. HMSO.

HAC 1986: 'Bangladeshis in Britain. First Report from the Home Affairs Committee'. Vol 1. HMSO.

HERTS 1986: 'Ethnic Minorities and Social Services'. Report of the Director of Social Services. Hertfordshire County Council.

HORN 1982: 'A survey of referrals from Asian Families to four social services area offices in Bradford'. E. Horn in 'Social Work and Ethnicity'. Ed. J. Cheetham (see above).

HOWE 1987: 'An Introduction to Social Work Theory'. David Howe.

IPR 1984: 'English Speakers only – a report of work on take-up of social security benefits with people whose first language is not English'. M. Tarpey. Islington Peoples' Rights.

JENKINS, RT. HON. R, MP. 1966: Address given by the Home Secretary on 23 May 1966, to a meeting of Voluntary Liaison

Committees. London, National Committee for Commonwealth Immigrants.

JONES C. 1977: 'Immigration and Social Policy in Britain'.

KHAN 1979: 'Minority Families in Britain; Support and Stress'. Ed. Verity Saifullah Khan. MacMillan.

LEEDS 1988: 'A Survey to Examine Communication Difficulties with Minority Ethnic Clients'. Final Report. Leeds City Council Department of Social Service. Information and Planning Section.

LESTER A. and BINDMAN G. 1972: 'Race and Law'. Pelican.

LMP 1985: 'The other Languages of England'. Linguistic Minorities Project. RKP.

LITTLEWOOD R. and LIPSEDGE M. 1982: 'Aliens and Alienists'. Pelican.

MAYER 1970: 'The Client Speaks: Working Class Impressions of Casework'. John E. Mayer and Noel Timms. RKP.

MHLG 1969: 'Council Housing, Purposes, Procedures and Priorities'. Ministry of Housing and Local Government. HMSO.

MSC 1986: 'Review of the Industrial Language Training Service. Final Report'. M. Nicod, A Jackson. Manpower Services Commission.

NCILT 1976: 'English Language Training in the Workplace'. National Centre for Industrial Language Training.

NISW 1982: 'Social Workers, their role and tasks'. (Known as 'The Barclay Report'). National Institute for Social Work.

NUGENT N. and KING R: Ethnic Minorities, Scapegoating and the Extreme Right in 'Racism and Political Action in Britain'. Ed. Miles R. and Phizachlea A.

PSI 1984: 'Black and White Britain': The third PSI survey; C. Brown. Policy Studies Institute.

RACK 1982: 'Race, Culture and Mental Disorder'. Philip Rack. London, Tavistock.

SCARMAN, RT. HON. THE LORD 1981: 'The Brixton Disorders, Report of an Enquiry. Home Office.

SCRRI 1972: 'Select Committee on Race Relations and Immigration Session 1972–73. Education, Vol 1. HMSO.

SEEBOHM 1968: 'Report of the Committee on Local Authority and Allied Personal Social Services'. CMND 3703. HMSO.

SMITH, D. J. 1977: 'Racial Disadvantage in Britain, the PEP Report'.

SRC 1987: 'Strathclyde Regional Council Urban Programme Evaluation Report, 195/79: Strathclyde Interpreting Service'. June 1987.

TAYLOR, S. 1977: 'The National Front: Anatomy of a Political Movement' In Racism and Political Action in Britain. Ed. Miles, R. and Phizacklea A.

TOSSELL, D. and WEBB R., 1986: 'Inside the Caring Services'. Arnold.

YOUNG, K. and CONNELLY N., 1981: 'Policy and Practice in the Multi-racial City'. Policy Studies Institute.

Index